Behind the
Counter

Behind the Counter

Fly Fishing
Tips, Techniques
and Shortcuts

Neil L. Jennings

Rocky
Mountain Books

VANCOUVER • VICTORIA • CALGARY

Rocky Mountain Books
#108 – 17665 66A Avenue
Surrey, BC V3S 2A7
www.rmbooks.com

Rocky Mountain Books
PO Box 468
Custer, WA
98240-0468

Library and Archives Canada Cataloguing in Publication

Jennings, Neil L

**Behind the counter : fly fishing tips, techniques and shortcuts / Neil L. Jennings.
ISBN 978-1-894765-92-3**

1. Fly fishing. I. Title.
SH456.J46 2007   799.12'4   C2007-902922-1

Library of Congress Control Number: 2007931971

Edited by Judy Millar
Book design by John Luckhurst
Cover design by Jacqui Thomas
Front cover photo Avid Creative, Inc. / iStockphoto
All interior photos provided by Neil L. Jennings unless otherwise noted.
Author photo by Linda Jennings

Printed in Canada

Rocky Mountain Books acknowledges the financial support for its publishing program from the Government of Canada through the Book Publishing Industry Development Program (BPIDP), Canada Council for the Arts, and the province of British Columbia through the British Columbia Arts Council and the Book Publishing Tax Credit.

Canada Council
for the Arts

Conseil des Arts
du Canada

BRITISH COLUMBIA
ARTS COUNCIL

This book has been produced on 100% post-consumer recycled paper, processed chlorine free and printed with vegetable-based dyes.

DEDICATION

This book is dedicated to my grandchildren, present—Mimi, Wesley and Zoe—and future. I hope you find the joy in the outdoors that I have. If you need a rod, give me a call.

Papa J.

CONTENTS

Where Would You Like to Go Today?: Travel Tips for the Peripatetic Angler

Do The Right Thing: Fishing Etiquette

Glossary

INTRODUCTION

I started fly fishing seriously in 1973 and have practiced that method exclusively since. From 1982 until 2003, I was a partner/owner in a retail fly fishing shop in Calgary, Alberta. During that time I was "behind the counter," answering questions and giving advice and counsel to thousands of fly fishers who came through the door. The clientele ranged from "wannabes" to some seriously talented anglers. Over the years I learned a lot about fly fishing, some of it by good example and some by bad. This book is a distillation of that experience. Most of the content of the book is in the nature of tips, tricks, shortcuts and techniques. A wonderful aspect of this sport is that you get to learn new things all the time. Because the learning experience is on-going, the curiosity quotient should stay high.

Before you begin, I offer this caveat. Much of what you'll read herein is opinion, mine, arrived at honestly. If you agree or accept my opinion on any matter, fine. If not, that's fine too. You be the judge. "Expert" is not a label I've ever aspired to. I sincerely believe that an "expert" is some S.O.B. who is more than fifty miles from home with a slide show he is prepared to show if you pay. I have seen more than my fair share of "expert" fly fishermen, some of them worth suffering, many not. Having read this far, you can decide if you want to suffer me. I've bought a lot of fishing literature over the years, figuring if I learned one useful thing from a book, it was worth the price of admission. It would please me if, whatever your experience in the sport, you find something here that proves useful or stimulates thought, discussion or debate.

Looking back, I see two objectionable interlopers in the sport—inflated egos and competitive anglers. A number of overbearing egos are present in fly fishing today, some in front of the counter and some behind. Most of these belong to people who have done little to distinguish themselves and nothing to justify their estimation of their own importance. The best reason to fly fish is that it is fun. You will not get to heaven faster by becoming a fly fisher, but the journey may be more enjoyable. So check the ego. As to competitive anglers, I believe they have entirely missed the point of the pursuit. They should take up golf or some other activity appropriate to keeping score.

A final note: I apologize for not employing metric measurement in this book. Fly fishing tackle in North America has always used, and continues to use, imperial measurement, not metric. For example, fly rods are 8½ or 9 feet long, fly lines are 90 to 105 feet long, tippet is measured in thousandths of an inch, leaders in feet, and so on. To prevent confusion, I have employed imperial measurement throughout. This is not a political statement, merely a reflection of common usage in the sport in North America.

Neil L. Jennings
Calgary, Alberta

What You Need: Basic Tackle

In my years behind the counter, probably the most commonly asked question was "What's it going to cost me to get into this sport?" Every time I heard the question, it put me in mind of the story about an investor looking to get into a new business. Applying due diligence, the investor first goes to the accounting department and asks the accountant: "What's two plus two?" The accountant replies immediately, authoritatively and somewhat indignantly: "Two plus two is 4.0." The investor thanks the accountant and goes to the engineering department. "What's two plus two?" The engineer thinks for a moment. "Two plus two is somewhere between 3.75 and 4.25." Thanking the engineer, the investor moves on to the computer modeller. "What's two plus two?" The computer modeller gets up from his desk, closes the door softly, turns to the investor and whispers: "What do you want it to be?"

Most tackle dealers (and fly fishers) will tell you that the basic set up for the sport is a fly line, a fly rod, a fly reel, some backing for the reel, a leader and some flies. This is the "two plus two equals 4.0" solution. A still more accurate answer will include such additional basic and necessary items as a fishing vest (or alternative) and accessories, raingear, waders, sunglasses and fly boxes. This is the "two plus two equals somewhere between 3.75 and 4.25" response. Beyond here, factoring in quality and feature considerations on the various components of the set up, you will inevitably come to "What do you want it to be?"

So let's take a look at the components one at a time. If you are an experienced angler, you may already know some of this, but a periodic return to basics is always salutary.

Fly Lines

As a general rule, fishing entails presenting a lure to a target which is usually some distance from the angler. Every form of fishing except fly fishing accomplishes this by attaching a weight (which may be the lure) to the terminal end of the line and then employing a rod to direct the weight to the target. The weight carries the line to the target. This is true whether you are spin fishing, bait fishing or surf casting. Fly fishing differs fundamentally because the lure in fly fishing (the fly) is weightless, or essentially so. Without weight, the lure cannot carry the line to the target. But in order to cast there must be weight somewhere in the system. In fly fishing, that weight is the fly line itself. The fly is attached to the line by a tapered leader, and the fly merely goes along for the ride with the line. *But make no mistake: it's the line itself that's cast.* And that makes fly fishing different from other means of fishing. The fly line is the cornerstone of the whole sport, and its importance cannot be overstated.

Simply, every fly line has a weight, a taper and a specific gravity. For practical purposes, fly line weight is designated by a number between 1 and 12. A #1 fly line is the lightest in weight, a #2 fly line slightly heavier and so forth up to a #12 fly line, the heaviest. The weight of the line is built into its front 30 feet by the manufacturer, employing standards of measurement agreed to by the line manufacturing industry. So every #6 line will weigh the same (within certain tolerances), regardless of who manufactured the line. Generally speaking, light lines (#s 1 to 4) allow the greatest delicacy of presentation, middle weight lines (#s 5 to 7) provide the greatest versatility, and heavy lines (#s 8 to 12) provide the maximum in power. Line weight is critical because every rod is designed to cast a particular weight of line.

As a fly line rolls through the air, energy is transferred and dissipated along the length of the line. For this to work properly, the line must have a taper built in—taper being a gradual change in the diameter of the line through the length of the portion being cast. The tapered shape of the line is built in by the manufacturer. The most commonly used taper in today's fly fishing world is the Weight Forward taper, wherein the diameter is smallest at the tip of the line, increasing progressively back to a position approximately 35 feet from the tip. All line weights can be purchased with a WF taper.

"Specific gravity," in reference to fly lines, is a fancy term which essentially asks, "Does the line float or sink?" Floating lines float because the manufacturer builds microscopic bubbles into the plastic finish, which give the line buoyancy. Sinking lines sink because the manufacturer puts lead or tungsten particles into the finish.

When I started fly fishing, and, indeed, when I started selling fly tackle, the world of fly lines was not terribly complicated. Lines were available in a relatively narrow spectrum of line weights and a couple of different tapers, and most of the lines would float. Today's marketplace, however, is absolutely filled with fly lines of every conceivable description and designation. You can buy fly lines of every weight; you can buy lines that not only sink, but do so at different rates; you can buy hybrid lines (mostly floating with sinking tips), and what's more, of various length and sink rates; you can buy fly lines with interchangeable tips for different fishing situations; you can even buy lines designed for specific species of fish. The permutations and combinations are enough to give a computerized inventory system heartburn. Manufacturers have filled every possible fishing situation niche with an offering of the "perfect" line. Have they done us a favour? I'm not sure.

Much of this proliferation of lines is probably overkill, and it certainly can be confusing. I am somewhat skeptical as to whether specialty lines are really worthwhile or merely an attempt by line manufacturers to get us to buy more things we really don't need. For example, I fish for pike with a fly rod and enjoy it immensely, but I do not own a "pike" line and feel no compulsion to. I suppose some of the specialty lines are of benefit, but I suspect many are not. Some of the advertised claims of the line manufacturers would have you believe that a particular line will add distance and accuracy to your casts. Some of this may be true, particularly in the hands of a very good caster. However, no line, in and of itself, will convert a poor caster into an accomplished caster, any more than a particular golf club will turn a weekend duffer into a candidate for the pro tour. If you want to add distance and accuracy to your casting, you'd be better served by taking a lesson from a qualified casting instructor—and some practice—than buying a new fly line.

Before rushing out and buying any of the specialty lines, consider carefully what you are trying to accomplish, and then be realistic in your expectations of that line. For example, a few years ago, several line manufacturers came up with a transparent fly line that they advertised as the "must have" line for successfully fishing in lakes. It quickly found acceptance in the marketplace, probably because it was heavily advertised and seemed to make some sense—if the fish cannot see the line in the water, they'll be easier to fool. While this rationale seemed reasonable enough, I remained skeptical. So I queried one of our customers, a superb lake angler. He allowed that he had tried the line, but found it of no particular benefit, explaining that while the fish might not be able to see the line, neither could he. He felt the line hampered rather than promoted his success.

The angler's primary necessity is still the floating line. This most versatile of lines allows you to fish both floating and sinking flies. When purchasing a floating line, look for good quality, even if it costs a few extra dollars. A good quality line will cast with more ease and last longer than its poorer quality cousin. It's useful to remember that, of all of the items of tackle you require, the *fly line is where price most closely tracks quality.*

Once you have it, keep your fly line clean. It will perform better and last longer than a dirty line. Do not expose it to gasoline, solvents, insect repellents or extreme heat. All of these agents can damage fly lines permanently and irrevocably. Do not stand on your fly lines, particularly if you are fishing from a boat. Fly lines are constructed by extruding a plastic finish over a core material, usually braided Dacron. The extruded material will usually determine whether the line floats or sinks. Grinding a floating line under your feet in the grime that accumulates in the bottom of a boat will both damage the microscopic bubbles mentioned earlier, compromising buoyancy, and ruin the finish.

A line can be ruined in very short order by a grooved rod guide with a sharp edge. Check your rod guides from time to time to make sure they are not worn and thus grooved. Either visually inspect the guide or run a small piece of nylon hosiery through it. If there is a burr on the guide, the nylon stocking material will catch. If a guide is grooved, replace it immediately. Also check the so-called "line guard" of your reel. Grooved metal edges act like small knife blades on the fly line finish and could damage your line beyond repair. (Note that when you are pulling line off the reel, never pull it backwards and over the "line guard," an action that, performed repeatedly, will produce grooves. When pulling line off the reel, pull straight ahead, never backwards.)

The useful life of fly lines is limited. Most manufacturers estimate the average life of a line at about 300 to 400 hours. A fly line's life runs in direct relationship with the amount of use and care it receives. Fly lines are similar to tires in this respect. Driving 100,000 miles a year will wear your tires more than driving 20,000 miles a year. Nevertheless, the longevity of fly lines is amazing. Think about it: if you have 25 feet of line extended out of the rod tip and make a cast to extend the line to 50 feet, an extra 25 feet of line passes through the guides. If you then retrieve that 25 feet of line before recasting, the line has made a round trip of 50, 25 out and 25 back. Fishing slowly, you would probably make a cast every two minutes. That makes 30 casts an hour, with 50 feet of line passing through the guides each cast. Add it up and you get 1500 feet of line passing through the guides in the course of one hour. In a ten-hour day, you have put almost *three miles* of fly line through the guides. If you fish with the line only ten days a year, that is almost 30 miles of fly line through the guides in the season. I find that remarkable in itself, but even more remarkable is that the whole distance has been covered by the *same 25 feet of line* moving out and back. Little wonder that fly lines wear out; it is a great wonder they don't do so sooner.

Fly Rods

Over the years I have been involved in teaching thousands of students to fly fish. Most came to the classes with no preconceived knowledge of the sport or its equipment, just a latent interest in this fascinating activity. Probably the single most mysterious piece of the puzzle for most of them was the fly rod itself, particularly if they had investigated tackle beforehand. The marketplace offers such a wide variety of fly rods that the neophyte, and, indeed, the experienced angler, can really be overwhelmed by the choices. Fly rods are available in price ranges from forty dollars to more than a thousand. What's the difference? What is a reasonable investment? What am I getting for my money? Why are the choices so numerous?

As a start, it is best if you understand, at least in an elementary way, what modern fly rods are made of and how they are made. For purposes of this discussion I am going to assume that the best fly rods for today's angler are made from graphite material. Other materials, such as fibreglass or split cane, are either obsolete, generally unavailable or too expensive, and consequently do not merit much consideration.

Graphite, as the word is used by rod manufacturers, is a generic term referring to synthetic fibres developed by the aerospace industry. Most people assume that all graphite is the same. Not so. The term is used to refer to many different but similar kinds of fibres. For instance, one manufacturer of graphite material for the automobile, aerospace and sporting goods industries makes over thirty different kinds (grades) of graphite. Lower grades are referred to as "commercial," and higher grades, "aerospace." Though properties vary among the graphite grades, all these grades have certain properties suitable for tubular fly rods.

To build a fly rod you must first build a rod blank—the shaft of hard graphite to which are fitted a reel seat, handle and guides. First the rod manufacturer designs and manufactures a solid steel mandrel. The mandrel is tapered to be thicker at the butt and thinner toward the tip. This mandrel will form the inside diameter and taper of the finished fly rod. A mandrel is built for each section of a fly rod. So, a two-piece fly rod requires a butt and a tip mandrel, while a four-piece rod is made with butt, mid-butt, mid-tip and tip mandrels.

Next, the manufacturer prepares a graphite cloth. Strands of graphite, lined up parallel to each other on the longitudinal axis, are laid in a special epoxy resin system (matrix) to form a cloth. The matrix keeps the graphite fibres in place. The graphite cloth is then cut in the shape of a long wedge, called a "flag." The flag is attached to one edge of the mandrel and the mandrel is rolled. The flag wraps around the mandrel, overlapping itself. Heat shrink tape is then applied over the flag, and the loaded mandrel is placed in an oven and baked at high temperatures. The baking process fuses the resins, rendering a hard piece of graphite material.

When baking is complete, the heat shrink tape is removed from the outside and the mandrel extracted from inside. What is left is a hard, hollow, tapered tube of graphite material, one piece of the rod blank. (The ferrule section—where the rod pieces join—may be formed as part of the mandrel or added to the blank after the baking process.) Most blanks are then sanded to remove the ridges left by the heat shrink tape. A hard finish is applied, for cosmetic reasons only, as most manufacturers believe the smooth shine more appealing to the consumer. Once the tip and butt are finished, along with a ferrule to join them, the blank can become a fly rod—with the application of a reel seat, a handle and guides.

While somewhat simplified, this, in a nutshell, is how tubular graphite rod blanks are made—regardless of who makes them. Though all rod blanks are manufactured in roughly the same way, they're not all the same. The type of graphite, while important, is only one variable in the outcome of the final product. Blanks display different properties depending on a number of factors: the design of the taper of the mandrel; the type of graphite; the kind of resin systems used to manufacture the blank; the care with which the mandrel is designed and manufactured; the care with which the blank is manufactured; the research and development that led to the design; the experience of the rod designer; and the quality of the fittings employed in the final construction. At one time, two of the top rod manufacturers in the world used the same type of graphite (known as IM6) to build their fly rods. Despite the same raw material, their products exhibited the proverbial "chalk and cheese" difference in their casting "feel."

This enormous variation accounts for the large spread in retail pricing for graphite rods. Inexpensive graphite rods, generally made with cheaper, commercial grades of graphite, are usually made in Asia, finished with inexpensive fittings, and delivered in cellophane wraps rather than protective rod tubes. Their guarantees and warranties are limited. Cosmetically they are not that attractive and are available only in a limited range of lengths and line weights. Replacement rod pieces are generally unavailable. The quality control in the original factories is not usually the best. In fact, I have seen "nine-foot" rods from one such manufacturer that, displayed on a rod rack, showed obvious variations in length. This is not to say, however, these rods are worthless. Some of them are adequate casting tools, though you might have to search with some diligence to find which are worthwhile.

Moderately priced fly rods generally are made in North America with higher quality graphite and fittings. Usually delivered in some kind of protective case, whether plastic or aluminum, these rods' warranties also will be sturdier, and you'll likely be able to find a replacement if you break a tip or butt. Generally more attractive in appearance, these rods will be finished with more care and attention to detail than the less expensive ones. And they'll come in a wider variety of lengths and line weight choices. Typically, rod manufacturers constantly try to improve their offerings by on-going research and development. When a new product line is developed, the new product becomes the pinnacle of the manufacturer's offering, and what used to be the pinnacle product falls into the moderately priced sector of the offering. Consumers are thus offered yesterday's best product, with somewhat cheaper fittings, for a significantly lower entry price. This has the salutary effect of making these mid-priced rods quite often the best value when considering quality for price.

Top of the line rods will offer you everything the art and science of rod design can deliver. Very attractive to the eye, they'll come with extensive guarantees and warranties and reflect the latest in rod design and technology. Such rods will come in an even wider variety of length and line weight combinations for chasing everything from panfish to marlin—and they're a joy to own and to fish. They'll also be costly. In today's marketplace, selection is limited only by the size of the potential purchaser's wallet and desire to shop around.

In the final analysis, the quality of offerings varies considerably, and price may reflect quality. You are not simply "paying for a name." If someone suggests you are, I'd suspect they're trying to sell you another rod they like, manufacture or represent.

When selecting a fly rod, *the single most important thing to bear in mind is how it casts.* After all, a fly rod has only two things to do in life—cast fly line and fight fish. Until you have done one or both with the rod, you have no way of knowing what you are dealing with. Moreover, there is nothing that you can do inside a shop to get the information that you require. Over the years, I've seen people in my shop do some remarkable things to fly rods. They wiggle them, flex them, bend them against the ceiling, bend them against the floor, sight down them like rifles, hold them to determine some critical balance point, even try to turn them into hula hoops. None of this will tell you, the potential purchaser, what you need to know. Nothing on the internet will give you the information you require. Nor will advertising. Nor even your friend (read also father, brother, mother, sister, priest). Do not assume what they like will satisfy you. What you need to determine is, "How does this rod cast in *my* hand and how do *I like* its feel?" Only one way to tell—cast before you buy.

In truth, a fly rod without the proper fly line attached is not a complete entity. As my erstwhile business partner, Jim McLennan, once remarked: "A fly rod without a fly line is like a guitar without strings." Jim's analogy is absolutely accurate. If you went to a music store and were faced with a row of stringless guitars, how could you make a cogent choice? The answer is you couldn't, because a guitar without strings is not really complete. In order to choose the right guitar, you would demand that the proper strings be attached so you could hear the instrument. Why do less when choosing a fly rod? The only way you can choose the rod that is right for you is to add line, take it outside and cast it.

Another commonly asked question in the shop and, indeed, on bulletin boards on the internet, is framed as follows: "Which is better, an Orvis or a Sage rod?" (You could substitute any rod manufacturer's names here.) My usual answer is: "Which is better, Chinese or Italian food?" (Substitute any ethnic cuisine.) There is no axiomatic answer to such a question. The answer can be nothing other than opinion, and that opinion is of no material consequence to your decision about which rod *you* like best. Over many years as an instructor of fly casting I've always made sure students have access to several different rods over the course of a session. If a student, even a complete novice, casts as few as two rods, he or she will have a preference. This preference arises not from anything the instructor says, but because even a beginner can feel differences. This is not to say that all beginners like the same rod. They don't. There is simply no right or wrong to rod preference. End of story.

Putting Rods Together and Taking Them Apart
Graphite ferrules are not like metal ferrules, such as you might find on a bamboo, fibreglass or spinning rod. To seat a metal ferrule, you first line up the guides on the rod sections, and then insert the male member of the ferrule into the female member and push straight ahead. That is not the way you seat a graphite ferrule. To properly join a graphite rod, first insert the male ferrule into the female with the guides on the two sections mis-aligned at about a 60 degree angle. Then push and twist the two sections together until the guides on both sections line up. (Note that most graphite rods have spigot ferrules. These ferrules, designed to allow for wear over time, do not allow the rod sections to actually meet. Do not attempt to get them to meet. If you do, you could damage the ferrule or have trouble later getting the sections apart.)

The pushing, twisting motion is necessary to properly lock a graphite ferrule. If you simply line up the guides and push the two pieces straight together, the rod will not be joined properly and the joint could separate when you cast. In this case, the very least that can

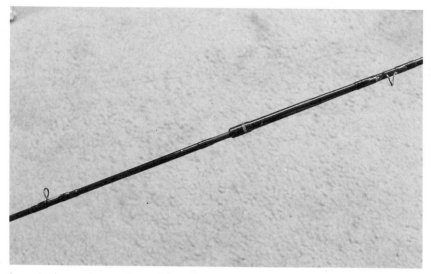

Insert the male member of ferrule into female with the guides misaligned at about 60 degrees, then push and twist to align the guides.

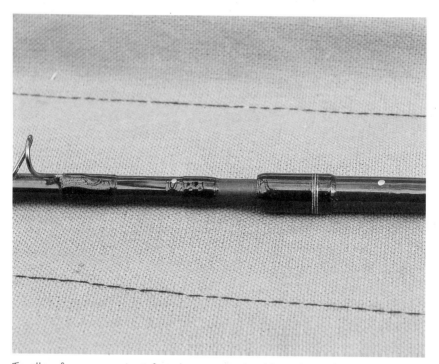

To allow for wear, spigot ferrules are designed so the rod sections do not actually meet.

happen is that the rod tip will be cast away. A nasty shock, but it can be recovered, assuming you still have a fly attached to the leader and the fly hangs up in the guides on the roaming tip. In the worst case, however, you could break the ferrule on the rod. It's not uncommon for a ferrule to shatter when rod sections drift apart during a cast—an easily avoided occurrence.

When taking a rod apart, the first thing to do is check the surrounding area to make sure you have sufficient room to work without the rod pieces bumping nearby obstructions. In one hand held about mid-chest level, grasp the butt section of the rod near the ferrule. *Fully extend the other hand* to hold the tip section of the rod above the ferrule. Holding the tip section steady, twist and pull on the butt section until the rod comes apart. This way, because you are already holding the tip section at full extension, the ferrule connection will come apart without the tip section jumping away from you.

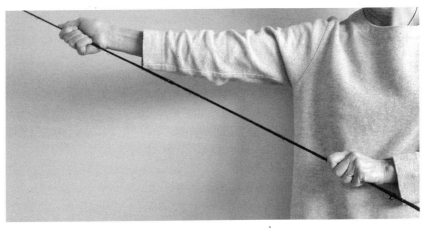

If you hold the tip section at full extension, the rod sections will part without mishap.

Unfortunately, people seldom seem to take rods apart this way. Most people grab the rod and hold it near the centre of their chest, hands close together on each side of the ferrule and give a mighty heave. When the rod separates, the hand holding the tip section jumps wildly back and away at some velocity. As the hand flies backwards, the rod tip jams into any nearby obstruction, usually resulting in a broken tip. And another unnecessarily broken rod.

Rod ferrules should be lubricated from time to time with paraffin wax. If you have ever seen an old-timer put a rod together, you might

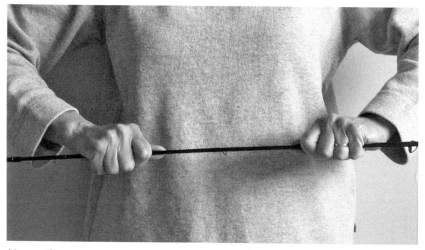

Above: By grasping the rod with hands close together, you invite a broken tip when the hand on that section rebounds suddenly.

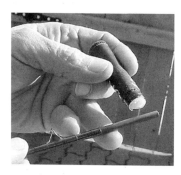

Left: From time to time, lubricate rod ferrules with paraffin wax.

Below: To detach a truly stuck rod, place it behind your knees, one hand each side of the ferrule. Force knees outwards, while twisting and pulling with your hands.

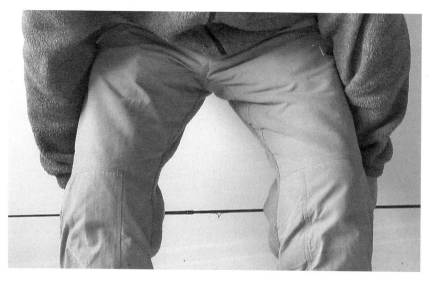

have seen him twirl the male end of the ferrule next to his nose, using a little skin oil to lubricate the ferrule. Do not adopt this practice. Over time, the oil from your skin can damage even a brass ferrule. Sometimes ferrules get so stuck that you have difficulty separating the rod sections. If this happens, there are a couple of things you can do. First, make sure you have lots of room. Crouch slightly and put the rod behind your knees, one hand on either side of the ferrule. Start with your knees close together and then force them outwards, pressing on your forearms while twisting and pulling on the rod sections with your hands. This tactic will usually do the trick.

If the ferrule is still stubborn, enlist the help of a companion. The two of you grasp the rod such that you *each* have a hand on *each* side of the ferrule. Then, in unison, pull and twist to get the rod apart. I have seldom seen a ferrule that would not part using one of these techniques.

Stringing a Rod

Most fly fishers know that the easiest and most efficient way to string a rod is to pull about 15 feet of line off the reel, rest the butt of the rod on the ground, double over the line/leader connection and then feed the doubled connection through the guides, moving up the rod. However, you should be aware that there is one more important step in the process. When you reach the tip guide with the doubled connection, it is critical that you pull the line and leader straight out of the rod tip.

Do not pull down or at an angle. If you do, you risk cracking off the tip of the rod. Why? Because you are now invariably holding the rod by the tip section, near the second snake guide down from the tip guide. When you pull the line/leader connection down or at an angle, the rod, restrained by your hand, is prevented from bending naturally below your hand and may break. When the Sage Manufacturing Corporation introduced its RPL series a number of years ago, users reported a significant amount of tip breakage. Almost all breaks occurred near the second snake guide—that is, exactly where most people would be holding the rod when stringing the line through the tip guide. After interviewing a large number of users, the rod design folks at Sage determined that breakage was most often occasioned by a user who made the mistake of pulling the line down, rather than straight out.

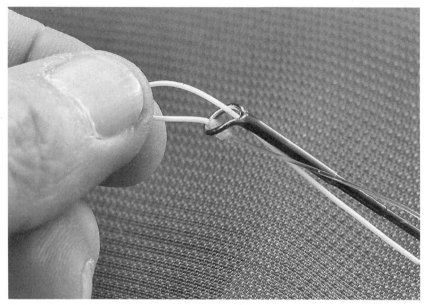

To avoid breakage when stringing a rod, pull line and leader straight out of the rod tip.

I Hate Hook Keepers

A hook keeper is that little ring or wire loop attached to the rod just in front of the grip. The idea is you put your hook in that ring or loop, then reel up the line tight so the hook does not dangle loose when you walk somewhere with the rod. I hate hook keepers, and I don't use them. Ever. Rod manufacturers always put them on trout rods, but oddly enough, almost never on rods of line weights #8 and heavier. I don't know why that is, but I wish they would just do away with the things altogether. Hook keepers do not solve any problems, and cause several.

If you are using a leader that is as long or longer than the rod itself—which most of us usually do—when you put the hook into the hook keeper and tighten the line, the line/leader connection will end up inside the guides on the rod tip. This poses a problem because the connection must be retrieved from the rod tip before you can make a cast. This usually involves putting the rod butt on the ground and pulling the leader straight out of the tip. (Be careful to not pull down on the leader, for reasons mentioned in "Stringing Rods.") The safest way to extract the line/leader connection is to put the rod down, but that is a nuisance I choose to avoid.

In my view, hook keepers cause more problems than they solve.

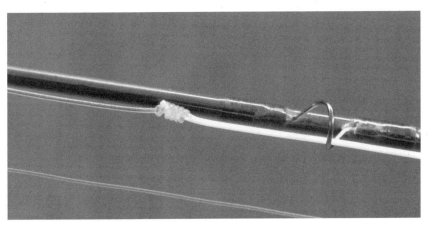

Hook keeper problem 1: the line/leader connection ends up inside the tip guides and must be retrieved before a cast.

The other problem with hook keepers is that when the line/leader connection disappears inside the tip guide and you tighten up the line, the butt section of the leader, folded around the tip guide, can get kinked at the rod tip. Putting a kink into the butt of the leader is not recommended because that section of leader, being the greatest diameter, is the hardest part from which to remove a kink. If you kink the butt section and do not remove the kink efficiently, the leader will

Rather than a hook keeper, hang your fly on a snake guide and take the leader around the reel foot before tightening. The line/leader connection will remain outside the rod guides.

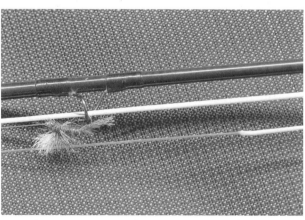

not straighten properly, but will fall off at peculiar angles. Even if you don't use it for its intended purpose, a hook keeper hanging around can be maddening, in that the line will sometimes jump up and half hitch itself on the hook keeper when you are casting. This drives me crazy and prompts its removal from my rods.

For these reasons, I don't use hook keepers and don't recommend them. A better system is to hang your fly on a snake guide near the fer-

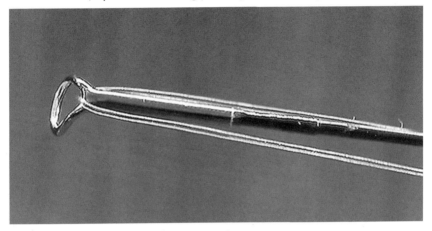

Hook keeper problem 2: the butt of the leader folds around the tip guide and gets kinked at the rod tip.

rule of the rod then take the leader around the reel foot before tightening the line. This system will ensure that the line/leader connection is outside the guides on the rod tip and is not getting kinked.

When you want to cast, merely release the tension on the leader by pulling some line off the reel, then remove the leader from around the reel foot, free the fly from the snake guide and make the cast.

Rod Care

After you have made the investment necessary to obtain good equipment, make a habit of caring for it. Easy to say, but it seems few people actually do it consistently. Over the years I have seen rods ruined or damaged by being stepped on, driven over, jammed into the ground, poked into trees, slammed in doors, smashed by trunk lids, fractured by flying lead weights, severed by ceiling fans and broken on boat gunwales. I know of two instances of rods eaten by vacuum cleaners! In both cases the rods were leaning in a corner, the leader dangling on the floor, right up until the vacuum sucked the leader, followed by the rod tip, into the machine. In fact, I think I can say categorically that there is no way you can think of to break a rod that hasn't already been accomplished, and it's nearly always a case of negligence or neglect. Making a conscious effort to create good habits when it comes to tackle care will be amply rewarded.

If you have purchased a rod with a guarantee that covers breakage however caused, that is good for you. But bear in mind that breaking the rod will inconvenience you while it is returned to the manufacturer for warranty replacement. Your best course of action is to prevent breakage in the first place.

Never lay a fly rod on the ground. If you do, it will get broken. You will step on it, your buddy will step on it, the horse will step on it, the car will drive over it. A rod on the ground will be broken. If you are going to put a rod down, stand it next to a tree or bush and see to it that small branches will cradle the rod in an upright position, even if the wind is blowing. If the rod falls on the ground, it will get broken. *Never* lean a rod against a vehicle. The sides of vehicles are slick and smooth, and even a slight breeze will cause the rod to slide off and wind up on the ground, where it will be broken.

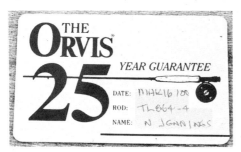

Rod guarantee card

When you are walking anywhere with a rod, always walk with the rod butt facing forward and the tip backwards. This will allow you to negotiate even thick cover without getting the rod hung up in trees and bushes. *Never* carry a rod with the tip facing forward. The tip will stab into something hard or jab the ground as you walk, and the rod will break.

When you make an errant backcast and get the fly hung up in an obstruction such as a tree or stream-side bushes, do not use the rod as a lever to extract the fly. Whipping the rod forward forcibly will only cause the rod tip to break. A rod will bend, but it wants to be straight. If you keep hammering at a bent rod, under repeated sharp loads it will likely break—your fault, not the rod's. If you cannot go back and extract the fly by hand, point the rod at the obstruction, keep the rod straight and pull on the fly line until the leader breaks or the fly lets go of the obstruction. *During this process, turn your head away from the place the fly is hung.* You do not want the fly to come loose and whiplash your face.

One of the most amazing rod breakage stories I ever heard involved a fellow who was fishing off a houseboat. Having caught his fly and/or line in some underwater snag, he yelled to his wife to crank up the engine and drive the houseboat away from shore while he maintained a death grip on the rod handle. Needless to say, the rod snapped before the boat moved very far. More amazing still, the fellow returned the rod to the shop, candidly explained the circumstances and demanded a replacement rod under warranty. It apparently had not occurred to him he'd done anything untoward.

Never put a rod on the roof of a vehicle. You will drive away and lose it. More rods and reels are lost from the roofs of vehicles than any other way. We had one unfortunate customer who lost five outfits (rods/reels/lines) in one fell swoop by putting them on top of the vehicle while loading his boat at the end of a float trip. After loading, he promptly drove out of the ramp and up a hill. By the time he remembered where he had put the outfits they were no longer there, and search as he might back down the hill, none was ever found—at least by him. If you are going to put a rod on a vehicle for any reason, put the rod on the *hood* of the vehicle. If the rod is on the hood, you will know its whereabouts before you drive away.

If you are finished with a rod for the day (or for even a short time), put the rod into a protective tube. If the rod is worth owning, it is worth protecting. All high quality rods come with rigid protective cases, and you should use them. If a change in your fishing venue during the day involves a drive to a new location, take the rod apart and put it away properly in its protective tube before you move. *Never* put an assembled rod into a vehicle. This practice is inviting disaster. Something—the spare tire, jack, tackle bag, cooler, waders or any number of other things—will fall on and break it. In one instance I know of, the tip of an assembled rod was broken off when the refrigerator door inside a camper popped open in transit.

Second only to doors (be they screen or automobile), the windows of station wagons and sport utility vehicles are particularly effective rod snappers. Here's how it works: the butt of a rod is placed on the dashboard with the rod extending backwards to the rear of the vehicle. Invariably someone pushes the rear window lift activator button,

If you must put your rod on a vehicle, place it on the hood, where you will see it before you drive away.

Put your rod in a protective tube when not in use, even for a short time.

the window rolls up and decapitates the rod. I know of one case in which three rods were simultaneously destroyed by this process. Get into the habit of casing your rod when it is not in use and avoid such disasters. I know of a cased rod run over by a car that remained intact, although the case was a lot worse for the experience.

Before putting a rod away, make sure it, along with the rod sock it goes into, are dry. Putting a wet rod or rod sock into a capped case invites mildew. Rods can be ruined by wet storage. The reel seat might corrode, and the guide wraps will almost surely discolour and be damaged by mildew. If you are fishing in a rainstorm and cannot dry the rod and cloth wrap properly before putting it away, make sure you do so at the first opportunity after you get home. If you don't have a case for your rod, buy one or manufacture one using plastic plumbing pipe. The pieces for such a homemade rod tube are readily available and very inexpensive.

From time to time, check the guides on your rods for wear. They *will* wear, gradually, because the fly line is constantly passing through them. You can do a visual inspection for grooves or, better still, get a small piece of old nylon stocking and pass this material back and forth through the guide. If the guide has become grooved with wear, the grooves' sharp edges will grab the fine mesh. Replace worn guides immediately; those sharp edges can cause severe and irreparable damage to your expensive fly line. It is not difficult to replace a rod guide. If you haven't done it before, take the rod to your local tackle dealer and request he do it for you or instruct you how. This simple repair will be a great deal cheaper than replacing your fly line. It takes less time to ruin a good fly line on a worn guide than to install a new guide.

Be sure to check the tip guide for wear as well. If the tip guide is grooved, replacement is very simple, quick and inexpensive. Assuming he is not too busy with other customers, your fly tackle dealer should be able to do it for you while you wait.

Will That Be Four Pieces or Two?

Anglers often wonder whether they should buy a four- or two-piece rod. In my view, four-piece is most often the answer. When I started selling fishing tackle in the early 1980s, the Orvis Company, then our principal rod supplier, offered two eight-foot, four-piece rods. One cast a #4 line, the other a #7. That was it. Times have definitely changed.

In the 2002 season, Orvis sold more four-piece than two-piece rods for the first time in company history, a history stretching back to 1856. I suspect the story is similar for other top rod manufacturers.

Modern four-piece rods function as well as their two-piece counterparts, and have a great advantage in portability. It is simply less difficult to move four-piece rods around. You can put them in a backpack, strap them to the frame of a mountain bike, stow them in a helicopter without pilot complaint and pack them in luggage that would never admit a two-piece rod. (Before 9/11, you could take four-piece rods on airplanes as hand luggage, but not anymore.) I have used nothing but four-piece rods for some years now and never had any complaint with their performance.

Yet a myth persists out there that four-piece rods do not perform as well as two-piece rods. I suspect this notion originated in the days of solid ferrules. Since a rod would not flex through a solid ferrule, you would get a "dead spot" at the ferrule. Therefore, the fewer ferrules the better. But with modern graphite ferrules, this is no longer so. Even with three ferrules, a properly designed rod will perform just as well as a rod with one. I own four-piece rods ranging in line weight from #4 through #11, and I'm satisfied with the performance of all of them. In fact, I'd be willing to bet that virtually no one, casting blindfolded, could tell the difference between a four- and a two-piece rod of the same length and line weight.

You will pay a little more for a four-piece rod, a reflection of the extra cost of the manufacturing and handling of four mandrels and three ferrules rather than the two mandrels and one ferrule needed for a two-piece rod. The premium you pay for these extra steps, in my view, is usually worth it for the convenience.

Fly Reels

Fly fishers love fly reels. Hand a fisher a fancy fly reel, and he or she will handle it like the Hope Diamond, turning it over and over, admiring the workmanship, making the spool revolve, listening to the wonderful little clicking noises as though it were a symphony. Having reverently removed the spool, he or she will hover over the internal workings like a mechanic ogling the engine of a Porsche. Admit it. You have done this. I've seen it a thousand times. We love beautiful tackle, and fly reels are among the most beautiful stars in the tackle galaxy.

Generally speaking, a fly reel is a fairly simple machine: a place to store line. But it is so much more than just that. So when you look at reels, carefully consider the following: the quality of construction, the reel's capacity, its drag mechanism, the availability of spools, the reel's features and its finish.

Quality of Construction

The method and materials of construction usually determine a reel's quality and price. Fly reel parts are generally made in one of three ways: punched from sheets of metal and fitted together using screws or rivets; cast in a mold; or machined from a solid block of bar stock aluminum. Some reels are injection molded from various sorts of plastic material, but these, in my opinion, are generally not of a kind or quality to warrant much attention by the serious fly fisher.

The least expensive reels are made by punching the parts from sheets of metal and then screwing or rivetting the pieces together. These reels may work fine for a time, but are subject to failing rivets and screws falling out. If you are using a reel constructed with screws, it is a good idea to use Lock Tight or a similar product. These are a liquid material that basically cements the screws in place. Remove one screw at a time, insert a drop of the product and reinsert the screw, repeating the process with every screw in the reel's frame and shoe. Riveted reels will almost certainly come apart eventually, and there is no practical way to get them back together.

The majority of mid-priced fly reels are of cast aluminum. Molten aluminum is poured into a mold and allowed to cool and harden. Once cool, the reel is knocked out of the mold, machined and finished. These reels cost up to about $200 retail, depending on the finish and type of drag mechanism installed. Cast reels usually work very well and stay together better than those with stamped parts.

The very best reels are machined, or mechanically "carved," from a solid block of bar stock aluminum with computer driven lathes. The resulting reels boast fine tolerances—parts fit precisely together with no gaps to trap and damage fly lines. The reels tend to be expensive, but represent the best in reel construction today. All top-end reels are made this way. Most machined reels are also anodized (the metal protectively coated by a process of electrolysis) to prevent corrosion in salt water. Most of these reels have a disc type drag system.

Capacity

The capacity of a fly reel is determined by its physical size. For trout fishing, the reel should, at a minimum, hold the fly line you intend to use plus about one hundred yards of backing (braided Dacron or similar non-stretching material installed on the reel before the fly line to extend the length of useable line for fighting a fish).

Almost all fly reels come with a chart telling the consumer how much backing the reel will hold with any particular weight and taper of fly line (lighter lines taking up less space than heavier ones). Check the chart and make certain the reel you are considering will hold the line and backing you require. If you'll be using the reel for big game fish, bear in mind you'll need more backing than for trout, so adjust the reel size accordingly. I recommend using braided Dacron and gel spun materials, which do not stretch, for backing. Never use materials that stretch, such as monofilament line. While monofilament will stretch to a tremendous degree when put on a reel under tension, it also has a "memory" and will return to its original length when the tension is removed. This property can actually damage a fly reel spool.

Drag Mechanisms

The brake system of a fly reel, "drag" is simply an introduced friction that keeps the reel from over-spinning when line is removed from it. Drag can be achieved in a variety of ways, some more efficient than others. One common drag mechanism, the "spring and pawl" system, has been used by reel manufacturers for decades, and is found in many brands of reels, from high to moderately priced.

Inside the frame of the reel, a spring is locked into position by rivets or posts. Attached to the spring, a small, triangular "pawl" faces the centre spindle of the reel, forced in its direction by the spring.

Attached to the inside centre of the spool is a cogged wheel or gear. When the spool is locked into place in the reel frame, the point of the pawl engages the cog on the spool. The greater the tension on the spring, the harder the pawl's drive into the cog, and the greater the drag on the reel. Most spring and pawl reels have an adjustment knob that moves a yoke inside the reel frame. As the yoke moves, it puts more or less tension on the spring, thereby changing the drag of the reel. Cheaper spring and pawl drag reels might use plastic or hard nylon pawls. These pawls are functional, but will not last as long as the metal variety. Whatever they are made of, pawls are easily and cheaply replaced when they become worn, presuming the parts are obtainable.

Most spring and pawl drag reels actually contain two springs and two pawls inside the frame, although only one is at work at a time. Manufacturers build the two sets in, opposite each other, to make the reel ambidextrous; that is, able to be set up for either right or left hand winding to retrieve line. The pawl that engages is the one turned to face the direction of the spindle. A reel set up for right handed winding can be reversed to left handed by switching the relative position of the two pawls.

The least expensive spring and pawl drag reels may not have a drag

The spring and pawl drag mechanism has been used by many reel manufacturers for decades.

When the spool is inserted in the reel frame, the point of the pawl fits into the teeth of the cog on the back of the spool.

adjustment knob. The greatest drag these reels will ever have is what is present when the reel is new. As the reel is used, the springs fatigue and weaken, the pawls wear and the drag consequently decreases. Eventually, with no adjustment, the reel loses all drag and will over-run. (When a reel overruns, you get a backlash: a tight loop of line binds into loose loops and the reel locks up, breaking off the fly when the line stops running out.) These reels have a limited life and are best avoided.

In the last two or three decades a concerted move into salt water fly fishing presented fishers with the challenge of larger, faster and stronger fish. Spring and pawl drag reels just could not keep up, spurring the development of "disc drag" systems. These have become more and more common in the marketplace. Disc drag creates friction where two bearing surfaces press together, thereby keeping the reel from over-spinning. Disc drag mechanisms vary, their bearing surfaces taking a number of forms—cork to metal, metal to metal and synthetic material to metal, for example. Their common feature, however, is surface-to-surface contact.

The contact surface in nearly all disc drag reels is much larger than in a spring and pawl drag, and therefore more efficient. Moreover, disc drag reels virtually always have a drag adjustment, and the adjustment range is always significantly greater than that of even the finest spring and pawl drag.

Years ago, only the very expensive reels employed disc drag, but with popularity and demand came innovation and the availability of less expensive versions. While some really fine spring and pawl reels are still available, disc drag reels have certainly grabbed a significant market share, and spring and pawl reels have generally been relegated to the lower priced market. As the price of disc drag reels continues to drop, their popularity will certainly increase. There could come a time—probably sooner than later—when spring and pawl reels cease to exist altogether, except as collectors' items.

Most modern fly reels are built with an external rim spool, which means the outer rim of the spool turns on an internal frame. This allows the user to "palm drag" the reel when it is spinning, allowing the angler to effect additional drag by putting palm or fingertips against the moving rim of the spool. Many people like this feature, though I generally prefer to let the reel's drag mechanism attend to drag. Be careful with such reels, however. If you dent the spool rim, it will then bind on the internal frame of the reel and the reel will no longer run smoothly.

On disc drags, the bearing surfaces vary from cork on metal to metal on metal (both shown here) to synthetic on synthetic.

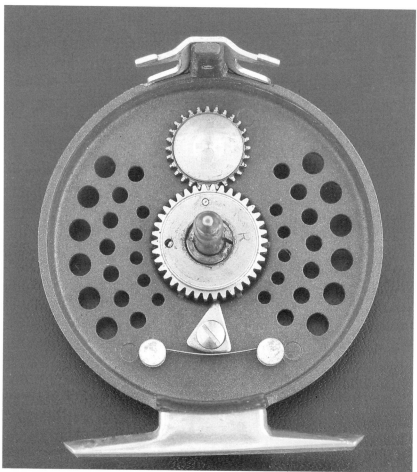

Spool Availability

Whatever reel you consider, make sure that spare spools are available for the reel. A spare spool usually costs about 50 percent of the reel cost. A spare spool allows you to house a second fly line—usually a sinking or sinking tip line—without need of a second reel to accommodate it. When you want to use the sinking line, simply remove the spool containing the floating line and pop in the spool with the sinking line. Even if you don't need or want a spare spool immediately, you'll want some assurance a spool will be available when you do.

A spare spool allows you to house a second fly line without need of another reel.

Features and Finish

The most popular fly reels today are direct drive, *single action* reels. The spool and handle are directly connected, so that one revolution of the handle causes the spool to make one revolution. By contrast, *multiplier reels* contain a gearing mechanism inside the frame or handle that makes the spool revolve more than once with each turn of the handle. You see them from time to time, but they have never met with much popularity. I would not recommend them. The mechanical complication is significant, and such complication usually leads to malfunctions. Indeed, the gearing mechanism on many multiplier reels is contained in the handle assembly, which is a separate piece on the reel. These handle assemblies have a nasty habit of coming off the reel at the most inopportune times—like when a fish is attached to the fly. When the handle assembly comes off, it usually drops in the water at the feet of the angler, never to be seen again. Once lost, you have no reel at all because there is no handle to wind the line onto the reel. Your fishing has just ended—until you get a replacement part or, better yet, a single action reel.

Anti-reverse reels have a clutch that allows the spool to turn and pay out line while the handle remains stationary. This means the handle on the reel will only turn in the direction required to retrieve line. So, if line is being pulled off the spool by a moving fish, the clutch will allow the spool to give up line while the handle stands still. Anti-reverse reels are exactly like spinning reels in this regard. Originally designed for use in salt water, the idea was that if a tarpon or other large game fish were running hard, the angler would not be endangered by the rapidly spinning handle of a direct drive reel. Unfortunately, like a lot of ideas that look good on paper, this one does not work out so well in the field. The problem is that the angler can be madly winding the handle on the reel at the same time the clutch is letting line go to a fast running fish. The angler is working hard, but retrieving no line at all. I was "sold" an anti-reverse reel when I took up tarpon fishing years ago. The first tarpon I hooked using that reel took off running and I, in my excitement, kept winding the handle of the reel until I was tired, all without retrieving a single foot of line. Neither I nor the guide could tell whether I was winning any line. The anti-reverse feature saved me from rapped knuckles, but took so much control away while fighting the fish that I had no desire to use this type of reel again. In fact, I returned it to the manufacturer and paid to have it converted to a direct drive reel. In my view, the anti-reverse feature should be avoided altogether. After all, it does not take an abundance of sense to keep your fingers away from a fast spinning handle, particularly after you are hit once.

Fly reels designed with a large arbor have become more available and popular in recent years. The arbor is the centre core of the spool, against which line is wound for retrieval. On a standard arbor reel, there is little difference between the diameter of the arbor and the spindle of the reel on which it runs. With a large arbor, there is a space between the spindle and the arbor, such that the arbor is a much greater diameter than that of a standard reel. This difference allows much faster line take-up. In fact, the difference in line recovery per revolution of the spool can be astonishing. If you are dealing with fish that run a very long way when hooked, like bonefish or steelhead, this feature is a decided benefit. *Large arbor reels* also have other advantages: line winds off and on in larger coils, so it is less likely

Large arbor reels have become increasingly popular because they allow for much faster line take-up.

to become tangled; the retrieval rate is high even with little line left on the spool; and the drag remains relatively constant even as line is removed from the spool, unlike a standard arbor reel. On the down side, large arbor reels are generally more expensive, they don't have as much line capacity as standard arbor reels of the same diameter, and they are, quite simply, big. In fact, a lot of anglers reject them for these reasons. I happen to really like them and recommend them because I think the advantages outweigh the disadvantages. And, if you ever hook a large bonefish with a standard arbor reel, I bet you'll agree.

There has been a virtual explosion in the past few years in the fly reel market. It seems that new reels are arriving almost monthly. At a minimum, a reel must have the capacity to hold the line and backing required and to pay line out smoothly, without hesitation, when a fish runs. It must also have a drag mechanism sufficient to keep the reel from overrunning when line is being removed from the reel at high speed. If your reel has sufficient capacity to hold the line and backing, turns smoothly, and does not overrun, it is doing what it is supposed to do. You don't require much more from a reel when fishing in freshwater for such species as trout, bass and pike. With big game species, however, the reel becomes much more important. When you are dealing with steelhead, salmon, bonefish, tarpon and other fast-running fish, the reel becomes a fish-fighting tool and it needs to be of sterner stuff.

Leaders

A leader is a somewhat invisible, tapered length of monofilament attached to the end of a fly line that separates the fly from the line. The subject of leaders can be a minefield, so I try to keep it simple. Over years of watching sales at the shop, I grew suspicious about how many anglers really knew their leader basics. Theoretically, in order to properly employ a 6X leader, your fly size should be in a range of #22 to #26—very small indeed. But we never sold anything like the number of these flies that would justify the number of 6X leaders that went out the door. So, either the customers were tying (or buying elsewhere) an awful lot of really small flies, or they did not really understand what 6X meant.

Leaders are measured and designated in two particulars—overall length and diameter of the tippet (small end of the leader where the fly is attached). The leader tapers from its largest diameter at the butt to its finest diameter at the tippet. Generally available in lengths of seven and a half, nine and 12 feet (though other lengths are available), the total length of a leader includes about 18 to 24 inches of tippet material of consistent diameter, allowing you to tie on a number of flies before the tippet material is used up.

Tippet material is measured according to its diameter expressed in thousandths of an inch, designated as "X," a notation which originated in the silk trade and watch-making about two centuries ago. 0X is defined as .011" in diameter, regardless of who manufactured the material. As the diameter of tippet material decreases, the number of "X" increases. Thus, 1X material is .010 of an inch in diameter; 2X material, .009 of an inch; 3X, .008, and so on down to 8X material whose diameter is .003 of an inch.

This measure of diameter is important because there is an optimal relationship between the size of tippet and size of fly you use, or even more precisely, between the diameter of the tippet material and the diameter of the wire from which the hook is fashioned. For a good strong knot when you tie on the fly, the diameters of the tippet and hook wire should be about the same. A large disparity means a weak knot. A larger hook therefore requires larger diameter tippet material, a finer hook, smaller diameter tippets.

To gauge the size of tippet you need, take the fly size and divide by four. The quotient will give you the tippet size, expressed in "X," that will work best for that fly. So, if you are using a #16 fly, divide 16 by 4 to get 4. 4X is the best tippet size to use on a #16 hook. There is some latitude, but this rule of thumb is generally valid.

To recapitulate, a leader, which separates the fly from the fly line, carries two designations: length and tippet diameter. The larger the fly, the larger the tippet material required. As far as possible, match tippet to fly size. If you are fishing Pale Morning Duns on the Bow River in early July, the fly size will most likely be #14 or #16. The Rule of Four says that your best tippet size for a fly of that size is 4X.

By the way, the "X" designation does not relate directly to the breaking strength of the leader material. 3X material from one manufacturer may be stronger than 3X material from another. Their diameters (.008 inches), should be the same; their breaking strength (and other properties such as stiffness, colour) may not. Remember that breaking strength should not be your most important consideration. Diameter is more important because it is directly linked to knot strength. Leaders are best stored in reusable Zip-loc bags with the leader designation written on the bag. Many leaders come packaged that way, so save the bags and use them when you change.

Check your leaders often for "windknots," simple overhand knots in your tippet that will diminish its breaking strength by as much as fifty percent. We call them windknots, but that is a misnomer. The wind does not put these little knots in leaders. They are a reflection of poor casting technique. Everybody gets windknots from time to time, so get into the habit of removing them when they occur. If you do not repair the leader, the fly will likely break off after the fish takes it, and you will be left with the unpleasant realization that you lost the fish because of laziness or oversight.

Keep your tippet materials fresh. Monofilament deteriorates over time, weakening from the outside in. Last year's sound 3X material might be only 5X strength now. You can not actually see such deterioration and will either have to test it or simply buy fresh tippet each season.

A leader will get shorter with each fly change because you are using up some of the tippet length to tie on each fly. Adding tippet material to repair a leader is significantly cheaper than constantly purchasing new leaders. How do you know when to add new tippet? Simply

Monofilament vs. flourocarbon tippet: the difference is clear.

align the line/leader connection with the tip of the rod and extend the leader to the butt of the rod. Most fly rods used today are about nine feet long, so you have a handy measuring device right in your hand. If the leader only reaches from the tip guide to the stripping guide of the rod, you probably need to add some tippet. Be sure to use tippet material that matches in size to the original on the leader when new.

One final word on tippet material. There are two types of material used for tippet these days—monofilament and fluorocarbon (see photo on page 36). Fluorocarbon material is relatively new and considerably more expensive than monofilament, but has some advantageous properties that may recommend themselves to you. Fluorocarbon material is said to be more abrasion resistant than monofilament, and it won't deteriorate with age. It has a specific gravity greater than 1.0, so it sinks slowly in water. But probably the most important difference between it and monofilament for most anglers is that fluorocarbon material has a lower coefficient of refraction, which means it is more transparent in water. The photograph on previous page, untouched or altered in any way other than cropping, shows identical flies suspended in water on tippet material. The fly on the left is tied on 4X monofilament tippet, the fly on the right to 4X fluorocarbon tippet, both materials made and sold by the same company. You decide which you would prefer.

Fishing Vests and Alternatives

A fishing vest is not an affectation; it is a serious piece of tackle. Too often, it seems, people approach the vest as a casual add-on purchase when buying their rod, line and reel, but a vest merits more consideration than that. Consider the vest a filing cabinet to keep your tackle organized and easily at hand. Here are some things to think about when choosing:

Make sure the vest fits properly. If it fits you when it is empty, it won't when you fill the pockets. As a general rule, get one size larger than your normal shirt size. If you wear a size medium shirt, you will want a size large vest. This helps also to accommodate a heavier sweater or fleece worn under the vest on cooler days. Don't worry too much about the front closure. Vests all have zippers or snaps, or both, but no fly fisher I know ever uses them.

Do, however, consider the material from which the vest is constructed. Many are a blend of cotton and polyester. These wear well,

Vest zippers should have large pull tabs to ease handling with wet or cold hands.

but tend to be heavier than those made of Supplex type nylon materials. Poly/cotton blends will not wick water as well as nylon and are more susceptible to mildew if not properly dried after a wetting. Nylon vests stand up better over the long run. Although more expensive, their longer life probably makes up the difference in price. Check the yolk of the vest for reinforcement. A yoke of Spandex type material will better distribute weight and be more comfortable. When a vest is full, it can be heavy, so this detail of construction is worth serious consideration.

All zippers—zippers are better than Velcro closures—should be nylon to avoid rusting, and their pull tabs should be large—easier to handle when your hands are wet and cold. If Velcro is used, make sure there is a generous enough amount to allow the pockets to close efficiently. And make sure your fly boxes will fit easily into the pockets. (Don't feel embarrassed to take your fly boxes with you to the shop when purchasing a vest.) If you have to fight to get the boxes in and out, you'll become frustrated and more inclined to ignore the closures.

It is imperative you get into a habit of closing all pockets after extracting what you want. The number of fly boxes lost from un-zipped pockets is legion. If you habitually leave pocket closures unattended, the fly box (or two or three) and contents that you inevitably lose will probably be worth more than the vest from which it fell. A good friend of mine once lost a fly box containing his previous winter's tying output of small nymphs—over 600 flies—this way, gone in one fell swoop from an un-zipped pocket. Luckily for him, another mutual friend found the box in the stream and got it back to the owner. You can bet my friend now makes a point of keeping pockets closed and writes his name, address and phone number on fly boxes.

The number of pockets will usually be reflected in the vest's price. More pockets mean a higher price. Think carefully about your needs in this regard. If you can get by with fewer pockets, do so. You'll carry less, and the vest will be lighter as you wear it over long distances and/or periods of time. As a general rule, I load the vest at the start of a season with everything I think I might need in the field. Periodically during the season, I make a point of emptying the vest and removing items unused to that point. Why carry things you don't use? Tuck them in a tackle bag or wader bag that goes with you when you fish. That way the items are nearby if wanted, but you don't burden yourself unnecessarily. Finally, decide where in the vest you are going to keep particular items and then keep them there at all times. Adopting this discipline will save your time for fishing the stream rather than your frustratingly disorganized vest.

While the fishing vest is the fly fishers' staple for carrying tackle, there are some alternatives you might consider.

One popular alternative is the chest pack, a small- to medium-sized pouch designed to strap to the user's chest. Such packs have slightly different configurations, but they have in common a variety of pockets for carrying fly boxes, leaders, tippet and so on. The chest pack is lighter than a vest, cooler in hot weather and quite comfortable. It's also easy to use, with everything hung in front of the user for easy access. If the angler is using a belly or pontoon boat as a fishing platform, a chest pack is generally preferable because a vest almost always hangs down in the water and gets wet. If the chest pack has a drawback, it's that it does not have the overall capacity of a vest. Most do not, for instance, have an adequate place to store a rain jacket. To address this deficiency, some anglers opt to use fanny packs or even

With plenty of room for the day's necessities, a backpack can be stowed nearby while you fish wearing a chest pack or vest.

Lighter than a vest, a chest pack is cooler and provides easy access to items, but has limited capacity.

The fanny pack has more room than a chest pack, but access isn't quite as convenient.

small backpacks to carry their tackle. The typical fanny pack has more room than a chest pack, but is not as convenient to use because the pouch is at your backside, and, to get at it with any facility, you have to swivel it around.

I really like the lightweight utility of the chest pack, but find the limited capacity less appealing. During the summer I often fish small streams, walking away from the car for an hour or so, then fishing back to the vehicle. The system I have adopted is to combine the chest pack with the backpack. The backpack allows me to cart raingear, a spare rod, lunch, water and camera with room to spare for the chest pack. I carry the backpack to the fishing venue, remove it, stow it in the bush and fish with the chest pack only. When I'm ready to move, I retrieve the backpack, stow the chest pack inside and carry on. I find this system works very efficiently. I have not abandoned the vest altogether, but when hiking and fishing I find myself using the backpack/chest pack system more often.

Raingear

Fly fishing is an outdoor activity, and you will eventually get caught in a rain storm. If you are prepared with good raingear, you'll be safer and more comfortable. Unprepared, you'll be, at best, miserable and, at worst, in some danger from hypothermia. Good raingear is not cheap, but it is essential for the fly fisher.

The cheapest raingear is made from a nylon shell coated with a waterproofing agent. This sort of raingear is relatively inexpensive, probably because it does not work very well. It may be better than nothing, but not by much. Because it does not rid itself of the condensation that builds up inside the garment, this sort of jacket can, in fact, become a hazard, getting you almost as wet as if you had no jacket at all. Once wet, you run the risk of reducing your body temperature and hypothermia can set in, even on relatively warm days during the summer months. This may not be a problem in short squalls or showers, but in extended or intense rains, cheap raingear will simply not do the job. I was once floating the Bow in June when a serious thunderstorm came rolling in, as they often do in that month. We opted to park the boat and hunker down on an island to wait out the storm. One of my companions wore only a treated shell. Even though he had the shell on well before the rain started, when it began in earnest he got soaked. His teeth began to chatter, and we had to row downstream in the storm in a race against hypothermia. By the time we arrived at the take out, he was becoming incoherent. We got him into the truck and wrapped in a sleeping bag to restore his body temperature, and he recovered. What had started as a wonderful day almost ended in tragedy, all owing to inadequate raingear.

The very best raingear is manufactured from either a breathable material or waxed cotton. The waxed cotton garments offer very good water repellency and also turn the wind. But they do have definite drawbacks. As a rule, they're bulkier and heavier than their breathable counterparts, which makes them more difficult to carry in a vest. They also must be maintained periodically by the reapplication of wax-proofing material. It's a messy job, yet if not done promptly and properly, the garment will cease to function as it should and become a liability. One time when I was pike fishing, a tremendous thunderstorm overtook us, raining copious quantities in a very short time. My waxed cotton rain jacket was past needing a fresh wax-proofing, and I got very wet, very quickly. To find some relief, I opted for a cold, wet hike back to the car. Though I used waxed cotton jackets for years and liked them, the bulk and maintenance problems eventually turned me to the breathable materials.

Breathable rain jackets shed the rain and wind while allowing water vapour and condensation to wick outward from the inside of the jacket, keeping the wearer dry and comfortable. They're lightweight and easily packed. The biggest downside is cost. In this case,

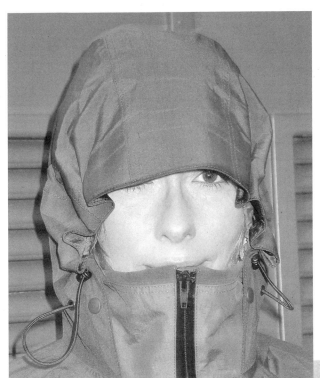

A well designed hood keeps rain out while maintaining your peripheral vision.

A good storm flap helps seal against wind and rain.

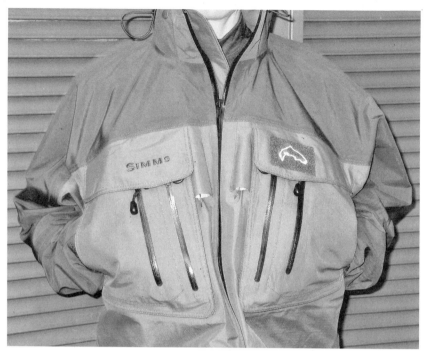

Handwarmer pockets are a bonus, particularly when fleece-lined.

Cuffs should have a gasket closure sufficient to prevent leakage.

for such a worthwhile investment in comfort and safety, I say damn the expense.

When considering a high quality rain jacket, check its features before buying. Do not assume the brand name or price tag will tell you all you need to know. The jacket should be large enough to cover you while you are wearing your fishing vest. If it is raining hard enough to need the jacket, you sure don't want your vest outside your jacket! The jacket should have a hood, and the hood should be adjustable to keep rain out while maintaining your peripheral vision. Some hoods are so poorly designed you might as well be enclosed in a cave. A properly designed hood includes sufficient adjustments to enable you to seal it around the face like a gasket, but still be able to see properly. A peak or bill on the hood is good for shedding water before it falls in your eyes. The jacket should have a storm flap down the front, with a waterproof zipper closure and/or overlapping snaps. The storm flap should extend all the way up to the underside of the chin, and some fleece material in the neck and chin area is a nice touch. Handwarmer pockets on the front of the jacket are a real bonus, particularly if they are fleece-lined. The jacket's cuffs should have some sort of efficient gasket closure to ensure water running down your wrists and arms does not leak inside the jacket. A drawstring at the bottom of the jacket is also recommended.

I prefer a rain jacket to be cut long enough to cover my upper body, but short enough that it does not drag continuously in the water when I'm wading waist deep. Large, bellows-style pockets and a rod holder on the jacket front are handy features too.

Waders

On those lovely, long, warm days of mid-summer, you might opt not to wear waders at all, preferring to "wet wade." This is a legitimate option. When I wet wade, I wear neoprene socks and wading boots. I do not wet wade in shorts, but prefer long pants to protect my legs from the sun and from twigs, burrs, biting insects and rose bushes along the stream. I use nylon pants, which dry quickly when I leave the water. Wet wading is a great option during part of the fishing season, but uncomfortable on rainy, cool days. Eventually you'll want waders.

Waders come in two basic lengths and two basic styles. Hip boots extend from the foot to the crotch; chest waders extend from the foot to about the sternum. The vast majority of fly fishers find hip boots too short, because they really allow the fisher to wade little more than knee deep before they fill with water. Chest waders are preferred by far because they allow for wading up to, and deeper than, the waist.

Waders come in two basic styles: bootfoot and stockingfoot. Bootfoot waders are one-piece units, with a waterproof upper welded to a pair of boots. You pull them on as you would trousers, except the trousers have boots attached to the bottom hem. Stockingfoot waders, on the other hand, consist of two parts: the waterproof sheath, which resembles tights or pantyhose with a sock-like end; and separate wading boots. You put on the stockingfoot waders, then slip your feet in the wading boots.

The practical difference between the two types is that bootfoot waders never really fit very well and stockingfoot waders do. The reason is two-fold. As one-piece units, bootfoot waders offer no choice in the size of the boot welded to the waterproof upper. Manufacturers establish boot size based on the "average" person. Thus, a medium size bootfoot wader will fit someone about 5' 8" tall, 160 to 190 pounds and who wears a size nine shoe. If you are 5' 8", weigh 215 pounds and need a size 11 shoe, you are out of sizing range for bootfoot waders. With stockingfoot waders, on the other hand, you buy a wader that fits your body and boots that fit your feet.

The second problem with the fit of bootfoot waders has to do with the shape of the human ankle and foot. When you slip your foot into a boot, its top opening must be large enough to admit the greatest diameter found in that part of your anatomy, that is, extending from the top of the instep to the heel. Then you wiggle your heel down into the boot. The problem: your ankle is always of a smaller diameter than instep to heel, so your ankle wallows around in the top of the boot. You have no ankle support. The consequence is quickly apparent when you try to walk on slick rocks in bootfoot waders. Stockingfoot waders do not present this problem, because the boot is opened up to admit the foot then laced up to the desired tightness for ankle support. The only advantage (to my mind, a small one) of bootfoot waders is you can put them on and take them off more quickly than stockingfoots.

The long and short is, you'll probably be better served buying stockingfoot chest high waders and wading boots to fit. Having made that decision, you then look at the material of construction in the wader.

Of all the advancements made in fly fishing tackle in the last 30 years, the invention of breathable waders ranks right up there with the invention of graphite rods, as far as I am concerned. In today's fly fishing world I would not consider buying, using or recommending any other kind of waders. They are the only comfortable wader in hot weather, and you can layer underneath them to make them utile in cold water. When I started fly fishing, the neoprene wader was just coming to the market, and everybody used them. But the advent of breathable waders killed the neoprene wader market, and for very good reasons. As soon as I used breathable waders I gave my neoprene ones away and made it quite clear to the recipient I was not doing him a favour. Some might argue that neoprene waders still have a place when the water is cold and conditions raw, and there might be some cogency there. However, unless you are going to invest in both kinds, get the breathables. Walking around in neoprene waders on a hot summer's day is a form of cruel and unusual punishment that probably should be considered unconstitutional. Since the arrival of breathable waders, the fly shop where I worked has not brought a single neoprene pair into inventory. Nobody wants them anymore.

Breathable waders are now available in a range of prices, bringing them within reach of practically all anglers. And there are certainly differences in quality and features among brands. One caution: it is imperative that you wear only wicking clothing under breathable waders. The breathable membranes used in the manufacture of the waders keep water molecules from entering the waders from the outside while allowing water vapour and condensation to escape from the inside. If you wear anything underneath that does not move moisture to the membrane, such as denim or other cotton garments, you defeat the whole purpose of the breathable membrane. Let's be very clear: if you wear jeans or sweatpants underneath, you might as well not be wearing breathable waders.

To make these waders warmer, dress in layers beneath them, and make each layer a wicking fabric. In cold water that might mean wearing wicking underwear, covered by fleece or pile pants. I highly recommend RiverTek garments from Simms Fishing Products (www.simmsfishing.com) and Under(Wader) Wear garments from Waterworks Lamson as clothing suitable for wear under breathable waders.

Wading boots, too, come in a wide array of prices, and the relative quality varies accordingly. You will be best served by a boot made of synthetic materials, not leather. Leather boots do not stand up well

The best wading boots are made of synthetic materials and have a felt sole for traction on slick rocks.

because, in the process of getting repeatedly wet and dry, the natural oils in leather are leeched out and the boot becomes hard and "set." After a season's use, most have to be soaked in water before you can comfortably put them on. Synthetics do not suffer from this problem. Whatever boot you settle on, try them on with your waders to ensure the proper fit. The soles of the boots should be made of felt to give you better traction on slick, algae-covered rocks. Rubber soles may be fine for hiking to the stream, but they are too slick in water to even consider. Some boots are available with studded soles, and the studs do give you better traction than felt on slick rocks. However, studded soles can ruin a good fly line the first time you step on it, and you cannot use studded boots in a boat. I would never allow anyone with studded sole boots in mine.

Sunglasses

If you are going to fly fish, you *must* have polarized sunglasses. Fly fishing entails the controlled flinging around of sharp objects, often in windy conditions. Eye protection should be at the top of your list of essential items. And lenses that are polarized cut glare on the stream, allowing you to see through the surface of the water. With polarized lenses you will see submerged logs before you trip over them, holes before you step into them and fish before you catch them.

Polarized lenses are made by sandwiching a polarizing filter between two layers of other material to form a laminated lens. To understand how a polarizing filter operates, visualize yourself standing in a room looking through a window covered by venetian blinds. If the blinds are partially closed, as in the photograph, you can still see outside by looking above the angled slats. That is analogous to how the polarizing filter operates. Light hits the earth and bounces up at

Polarized lenses work in much the same way as venetian blinds.

about 35 degrees. If not blocked, this bounced light creates glare, particularly on a shiny, reflective surface like water. The polarizing filter blocks that bounced light with a barrier not unlike the partially closed venetian blind. You can still see over the barrier, but the glare, cut off by the polarizing filter, does not reach your eye.

The quality of polarized sunglasses varies enormously, as does the price. For the most part, price depends the lens material—either optical quality glass, polycarbonate or acetate. Glass laminate lenses are usually the most expensive, followed by polycarbonate then acetate. Glass and high quality polycarbonate lenses are best, because they can be made with the least amount of visual distortion. Glass lenses are not as subject to scratching as the others, but tend to be heavier.

Polarized glasses sport a variety of lens colours. As a general rule, amber (yellow) or tan are preferred. These colours protect your eyes from bright sun, while giving you the contrast you want while fishing. They also work well in low light conditions, whereas grey lenses tend to be too dark. Some polarized lenses are photochromic; that is, the tint changes, growing darker or lighter to compensate for stronger or weaker light. I never cared for this feature, preferring instead to have constant density lenses.

If you require glasses for visual acuity, you can obtain prescription polarized glasses. Check with your optician or tackle dealer to see what is available. For those of us whose eyes are not what they used to be, there are even prescription bifocals. For those who do not want to invest in prescription polarized glasses, there are a couple of alternatives. Clip-on polarizing filters attach to your regular glasses, but do not work particularly well owing to some flaring between the filter and glasses. A better alternative may be one of the "fit-over" arrangements, a pair of polarized glasses worn over top of your regular glasses. I have used several types and they work well. Some say this arrangement makes you look like you just had eye surgery, but, as they say, looks ain't everything!

If you have a pair of sunglasses already, but don't know if they are polarized, you can take them to your tackle dealer and test to find out. Hold two pairs of polarized glasses close together as they would fit on your face and look through them. You should be able to see through both lenses. If you then turn one pair 90° to the other, the view will turn opaque and black out *only* if both pairs are polarized. You have effectively closed the venetian blind. If only one of the pairs is polarized, you will still be able to see through both lenses when they are crossed.

So get yourself some polarized sunglasses and use them. You will be amazed at what they do. Do not leave home without them.

Fishing Hats

I consider a proper hat to be an essential piece of tackle for fly fishing. Almost any hat will do if it gives the wearer some protection for the back of the head, neck and ears. It should also have some sort of brim on the front to help reduce glare from reflected light. The underside of the brim should be a dark colour for the same reason. I often fish in a cowboy hat, finding it provides all the protection required from sun, rain and flying hooks. If a leader comes too close, it hits the brim of the hat and follows it around without the hook hitting me. On hot summer days, I like a straw cowboy hat—cooler in the heat. These do not, however, protect from rain as well as fur felt hats.

Note that baseball caps need not apply for this job. Why? They do not afford any protection to the back of the head from flying hooks. If the leader comes close when you are wearing a baseball cap, you will probably also get to wear the hook. The only exception would be the "Foreign Legion" style, which have a cape of cloth that drops down from the back of the cap, and the "Up-downer" style, which has a long rear bill that folds down over the back of the neck. While perhaps not terribly stylish, either will protect you properly.

The cowboy, up-downer and foreign legion type hats all serve the purpose well, while the baseball cap does not cover the back of the head sufficiently to protect you from flying hooks.

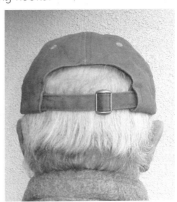

Flies

In the shop, I was often amused by the following recurring scene. A customer enters and asks: "What are they taking down on the Bow?"

Clerk: "There's a heavy Trico hatch every morning and some of the fish are really getting after them."

Customer: "Can you show me the right flies?"

Clerk (showing the Trico patterns in sizes #18 and #20): "Sure, right here."

Customer (moving away as though the Tricos were contagious): "Boy, are they ever small. I want something bigger."

What's wrong with this picture? The point of fly fishing is to offer an imitation of a food item close enough in size, shape, colour and behaviour to be accepted by the fish as another morsel of what it is already naturally eating. If the fish is eating small flies, the angler needs to offer a small imitation, whatever comfort level he or she might have with fishing the tiny fly. To do otherwise will probably mean going without a grab. Think of it this way: if you are going to eat corn flakes for breakfast, you will not be happy with one or two flakes. You'll eat lots to satisfy your hunger. By analogy, if it's eating tiny flies, a fish must feed more often and presumably over a longer period of time in order to become satisfied. Assuming you do not put the fish down by poor casting or a bad approach, when the fish are eating tiny flies, your odds are actually better.

Whether you're a beginner or experienced angler, fly selection is a puzzle. The number of fly patterns available is nothing short of astounding, and these numbers grow, literally, with each passing day. Fly patterns come into and go out of fashion, to some extent, so you'll be best served by checking with your local fly tackle dealer for recommendations. Circumstances vary with locale and season, and insects, like wildflowers, emerge at different times over the course of the year. If you wish to see prairie crocus, you'd best look in early spring. They bloom first thing and then fade away, leaving no sign of their existence until roughly the same time next year. For insect emergence times, your tackle dealer can assist with a hatch chart, which is an exposition of the historical times of appearance of insects on a stream or in a general locale, together with recommended patterns and sizes to match the emergences. Hatch charts exist for almost any river or locale where anglers chase trout.

So choose your flies thoughtfully and not randomly. The more information you have about current conditions in the place you are going to fish, the better your choices will be. Be innovative and prepared to change your approach if things are not working to your satisfaction. Remember, you are not the last arbiter of what fly to use. The fish you are trying to catch is. As a general rule, if you are fishing in waters that receive a lot of fishing pressure, your fly selection may be more critical for success. In my experience, hard-fished waters usually demand smaller flies and more careful approaches.

Most of us, with a kind of "you can never be too rich or too thin" approach, carry far too many flies, more than we could ever possibly use. Undeniably though, anglers do develop confidence in certain patterns, and confidence in a pattern often makes you fish it better. Thus success becomes a self-fulfilling prophesy, reinforcing the fly selection. Over the years, I have seen several articles in fly fishing magazines wherein the editors consulted famous anglers about their "seven favourite fly patterns" or whatever. It's interesting that the overlap of patterns mentioned is always greater than the disparity. But remember that fly selection is not the only important piece of the puzzle. Ultimately, your success has a lot to do with how you present the fly.

Random Casts: On Getting There and Being There

You're Going Where?

We all have our little secrets when it comes to fishing locations, but don't carry the secrecy to a ridiculous degree. Wherever you are going, let somebody know the general location and expected time of your return. Ironically, I will never forget my relief when one of my former business partners had his heart attack at the shop and not alone on some mythical "Frenchman's Creek," where nobody could have found him.

Organize Your Tackle

I have a very good friend and angling companion who appears to pack his fishing tackle in his truck with a shovel. That is the only way I can explain the general disorganization of the whole lot. I truly do not know how he finds anything amid the debris. I once happened upon him leaning into the rear of his vehicle, tossing out all manner of tackle onto the adjacent two acres of ground. When I inquired what he was up to, he announced he was "reorganizing" his tackle. As I remarked at the time, reorganization, by definition, implies some previous state of organization, a state I was unaware had ever been visited upon his gear. I suggest you organize your equipment in a fashion that makes it easy to go fishing yet difficult to forget anything you may want.

I use one duffel bag for vest, waders, wading boots, fleece, rainjacket, hat, spare glasses, camera and water bottles and another for rods and reels. If I leave the house with these two bags, I know I have everything I want for the day, with the exception of food. At the end of the day, each item used is returned to the appropriate bag. This system

Rod bag and gear bag. Organize equipment so that it's easy to go fishing yet difficult to forget things you may want.

saves a lot of time and can also prevent the catastrophe of arriving at the stream without some essential piece of equipment. Before I set off for the day, I take a minute to review a mental checklist of items needed. It is also a very good idea to take more than one rod on any outing. You do not necessarily carry both on the stream, but have a spare available. With only one rod, should some accident happen, your fishing is at an end long before you want it to be.

Hiking With a Fly Rod

I generally fish small streams in the foothills and mountains on foot. My usual procedure is to park the car, rig up, hike downstream for some distance and then fish my way back upstream to the car. If you are hiking any distance to or along a stream before fishing, I recommend you string the rod and attach a fly before starting your hike. Although you might occasionally get the rod and/or leader hung up on leaves, tree limbs and bushes, which is frustrating, it's nowhere near as frustrating as getting an unstrung rod hung up and having the tip pull off and disappear. I learned this lesson the hard way some years ago. My wife and I spent the better part of two hours carefully retracing our steps to find the rod tip that would not have been lost had the rod been strung while we were hiking. I have always considered that we were particularly lucky to have found the missing tip. A tree limb strong enough to pull the rod's tip off will usually catapult it into the bush beside the trail, never to be seen again.

When hiking and fishing both, I use a backpack to carry my gear. When I arrive at a place I want to fish, I stow the pack on the stream bank and leave it there until I move on. I also carry a spare four-piece rod attached to the backpack. Then, if the rod breaks on the stream, although I am not happy, I do have a spare to finish out my fishing day.

Observe Your Surroundings and Plan Your Approach

Approach a fishing situation slowly and carefully. Tread lightly, making as little noise as possible. If you charge down the stream bank to the water, the vibrations of your movements can alert and frighten all fish in the immediate area. A trout's lateral line is a sensory organ that picks up pressure changes and vibrations very efficiently. Fish often lie in relatively shallow water near banks, so don't frighten them before you even begin. It's a good idea to "get your line wet before you get your feet wet." Often you will find more fish at or near the bank than in more open water. If you dash into the water immediately, you'll probably spook some fish you otherwise might have caught.

Once you are in the water, wade carefully. Tripping over rocks or causing them to tumble can also alert fish. Noises underwater travel farther and faster than do similar noises through the air above. This is particularly so in quieter, slower water. Wade slowly, without pushing waves ahead of you. For a lesson in wading and approaching fish, watch your local heron.

Study your surroundings. I approach fly fishing as a series of small mysteries to solve; the more data and clues I can collect, the better. If you see stonefly shucks on the streamside rocks and it has not rained recently (which would wash the shucks away), you might find adult stoneflies in the streamside bushes. If you happen upon a spider web near the stream, check its contents to see which insects might have recently hatched. Are there insects in the air or on the water? What kind? Is there a lot of bird activity near the stream? If so, chances are they're feeding on hatching or ovipositing insects. Observations like these will help you properly select flies.

When matching flies with the naturals on the water, try to imitate size, general shape, behaviour and, perhaps, colour. Size is usually the most critical element. If you are getting refusals from rising fish, assume a smaller fly is needed. Try to catch a real fly for closer inspection, and compare it to your flies. We tend to overestimate the size of insects in flight; they are often not as big as we think. Observe too the behaviour of insects, which will tell you how to properly fish the imitations. The more your fly behaves like a natural, the more likely it is to be accepted by the trout as a proper stimulus to feed.

Carefully observe rise forms (the way the water moves when a fish takes a fly from the surface) in the stream. The rise form can give clues to what the fish are eating. Until full or disturbed, trout will stay in one spot, waiting for mayflies, which tend to drift in the same current "lane," to come to them. They then take the mayflies with a sipping rise, from the one feeding station. A splashy, slashing rise form would indicate the fish are taking caddis or some other insect that moves vigorously on the surface. Because these insects are so mobile, the trouts' rises don't usually occur in a single "lane." If a rise form leaves a bubble behind, the best bet is that the fish took something from the surface. Watch closely. If the rise form is made by the dorsal fin of the fish, chances are it is taking something just below, not on, the surface.

When casting to a rising fish in moving water, do not cast to the rise form. If you do, you are probably casting to where the trout was, not where it is. Here's why. The trout will see an insect when it drifts into the trout's visual window. As the insect drifts downstream, the trout begins to rise in the water to intercept the insect. As the trout rises, it is carried downstream by the current. At the point of interception, the trout has travelled downstream. The rise form will appear where the insect is taken, but after taking the insect the trout will move back to the position from which it originally started. If you cover the rise form and the trout has moved back upstream to his feeding station, your fly will land behind the fish and your fly line will probably fall over the fish and frighten it. In addition, the rise form itself is being swept downstream by the current, so casting at the rise form is taking the fly further away from the fish's location. In casting to a rising fish, place the fly far enough upstream of the rise form that the fish can return to his feeding station and still see the offering floating down to him as if it were a natural.

Your chances of catching a fish whose location you know will greatly improve if you move slowly, keep low and avoid frightening it with some reflection from your tackle. Avoid throwing a shadow on the water. Remember that refraction of light in water makes things under the surface appear closer than they really are. With some care and planning, you can get quite near a fish before making your cast. Then, before you cast, "check your six." That is, check behind you for any obstructions to your back cast.

Learn the habits and behaviour of the particular fish you seek. Different species of trout prefer different microhabitats. Cutthroat usually prefer to be in the flow. Rainbows prefer faster water than do browns. In a stream that holds both, the rainbows will usually be in the riffles and the browns in the pools or slower water near bankside. This is not a hard and fast rule, but true more often than not. The more you learn about your water and your quarry, the more consistently successful you will become.

Wading

Aviators have an expression: "There are old pilots and there are bold pilots, but there are no old bold pilots." While not as inherently dangerous as flying, wading has some of that flavour. When you are fishing, you are probably wading, and when it comes to wading, timidity is better than temerity. Do not become a bold wader or you will get into trouble. If a little voice in your head tells you *are* getting into trouble, believe it. And remember that bold wading will not necessarily bring better fishing.

When you do wade, go with the flow—cross fast water moving downstream and across at an angle. Move your feet one at a time, making sure your lead foot is firmly planted before sliding your trailing foot along at a 60 to 90 degree angle to it. If the trailing foot comes up beside the lead foot as if you were walking, your foundation is not as sound. Never cross your legs or feet when wading, which makes you a very unstable platform for the water to knock down. Wear a wading belt.

To cross a reach of water, plan your route carefully for both the crossing—and return—before you begin. Be especially careful wading at the downstream end of any island. This deposition zone for small pebbles and sand makes for loose and unstable footing. If you get too far off the downstream end of an island and try to wade back, you will be moving directly into the rush of water. That small gravel and sand may start to roll out from underfoot, and you could dig yourself into a lot of trouble. Avoid wading upstream against current unless the current is fairly benign.

If you do go in, do not panic. A popular misconception is that a pair of waders full of water are as good as cement shoes that will invariably send the wearer to the bottom to drown. This notion is reinforced by the media every time a wading angler meets a bad end. But it is wrong. The biggest danger of falling in is the panic it might produce. You can swim in full waders, just as you can swim if you fall into a swimming pool with your clothes on. True, water weighs 62.5 pounds per cubic foot, but only when exposed to gravity. Inside the water medium itself, buoyancy overcomes the law of gravity. If you fall in, position yourself on your back with your knees bent and feet extended downstream so you can push off obstructions as the current carries you. Angle to the nearest bank and dog-paddle to shore. When you get there, crawl out of the water. Once on dry land, do not try to stand up or you will find that

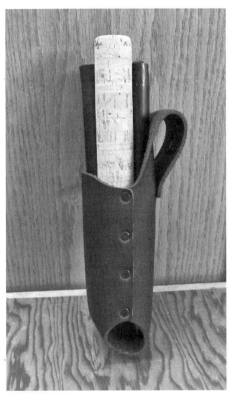

While sometimes pricey, a wading staff such as this folding version are worth it for the peace of mind they bring.

the water in the waders suddenly *does* have to obey the law of gravity. Instead, crawl out of the stream and in the process, crawl out of the full waders. Under no circumstances should you try to remove the waders while the current is sweeping you along. You will gain nothing by shedding them, and, in an anxious situation such as this, you don't want to do anything to reinforce the panic—like trying to doff waders that may be hard enough to get out of on dry ground. If you can hang onto your outfit when you go in, fine. If you cannot do so safely, let it go; they are making new rods and reels every day. Your object is to get out of the water safely. If the water is particularly cold, it is very important to get out quickly. Hypothermia is a very real risk if you are immersed for an extended period.

If you are unsure about wading, consider getting a wading staff. The staff can give you some measure of extra stability, like a third leg. A folding staff is far superior to a rigid one, which will always get in the way when fishing and attracts loose fly line like a magnet. The very best folding staff is the Folstaff, which features stout interlocking sections and an elastic cord running down the inside. Folded, it's about 10 inches long. It sits in a holster on a wading belt, to be extracted when needed. Once out of the holster, the elastic cord snaps the staff taut automatically. A number of years ago, I gave my wife a Folstaff for Christmas, and she contends it is the best piece of tackle she has ever used. Good folding wading staffs are expensive, but worth the peace of mind, and are, as my erstwhile partner liked to point out, cheaper than a funeral.

The "Just in Case" Kit

While the sport is not inherently dangerous, it is practiced outdoors in places that can be remote and rough. Sadly, accidents can happen. It's a good idea to be ready for such eventualities by taking some precautionary steps. When I go outdoors I always take a few items in the boat or car that I would rather have and not want, than want and not have. A "fall in the river kit" contains a dry, warm change of clothing for that day someone needs to get out of wet clothing sooner than their wet garments might dry. A basic first aid kit contains an assortment of band aids, bandages (including tensor type and triangular), gauze, cotton swabs, cotton balls, pain reliever, moleskin, waterproof tape, alcohol swabs and antiseptic and burn ointment. I have a friend who is allergic to bee and wasp stings, so when he is along I always make sure he has his EpiPen handy. A "space blanket" takes up little room and is invaluable in case somebody needs to wrap up and stay warm. Spare batteries, flashlights, waterproof matches, candles, eyeglasses, eyeglass screws, and small tools are also good items to include in the travelling kit. You hope you won't need them, but it's a good plan to have them available or nearby.

When you are going on more than a day trip, you definitely need to consider these precautions. If you are going in a boat, remember to take all the mandatory safety equipment required under prevailing local regulations for boaters, including an approved personal floatation device for each occupant of the boat, distress signalling device, whistle, buoyant heaving rope, waterproof flashlight, knife and bailing can. If you are unsure what items you need, check with local transportation authorities for a complete list. If you are using an inflatable boat, have a repair kit for the boat, and make doubly sure all items in the kit are current and not past their expiry date.

I also carry a few small items in my vest, such as alcohol swabs, Band-Aids, moleskin, headache tablets, antacid tablets, a butane lighter, Immodium, sunscreen and lip balm. These things take up little room, weigh next to nothing and can save a fishing trip.

Hooks

Barbless Hooks

There has been, and continues to be, a debate as to whether there is any material difference in mortality in released fish caught with barbed or barbless hooks. The argument has at times taken on a stridency akin to the debate over the right to bear arms. I am not terribly interested in this discussion because I made up my mind long ago that barbs are unnecessary and, indeed, problematic, particularly when they get stuck in anglers. I have used barbless hooks for all kinds of fish for many years and have consistently recommended them. They are easier to remove from both fish and fishermen, and I do not believe you will lose a fish simply because the barb has been removed.

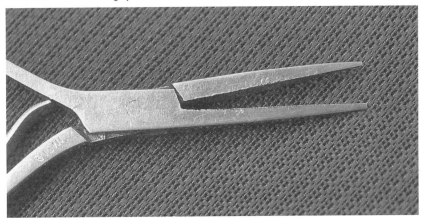

To mash the barbs on hooks, use flat blade pliers with no serration.

Many jurisdictions, in fact, have now passed regulations mandating barbless hooks for sportsfishing, so whether you tie or buy your flies, you will have to mash the barbs. For mashing barbs on hooks, it's best to use flat pliers with no serration. Approaching from the side of the hook, place one blade of the pliers on top of the barb and the other under the hook. Then squeeze straight down gently. The barb will flatten without damaging the hook. I find this method works better than forceps for barb removal. Especially on a large hook, forceps may not work terribly well, and may even damage the forceps.

Make Sure Hooks Are Sharp

In order to be effective, hooks need to be sharp. With the advent of chemically sharpened hooks, this is not usually a problem, at least until you run the hook point into a rock or some other hard object.

Check hooks for sharpness by putting the point of the hook on a fingernail and dragging on the hook. If the hook digs into the fingernail surface, it's sharp. If it skids, it requires some attention.

Stainless steel or salt water hooks are notorious for being dull right out of the box. Check all such hooks for sharpness before using or tying on them, since most are not sharp enough without some work.

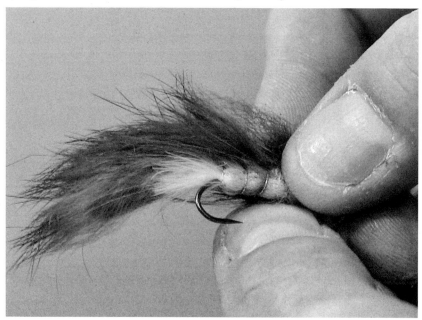

Test the sharpness of your hooks by dragging the point across your fingernail.

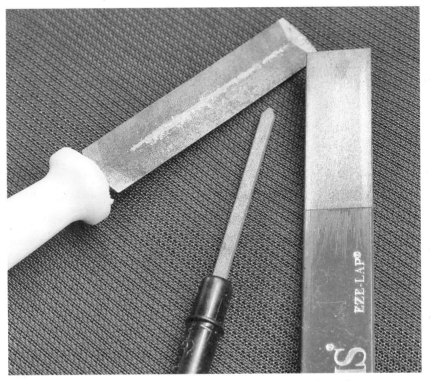

Various devices for sharpening hooks: from left to right, a file, a diamond-grit impregnated shaft, and diamond-grit flat. Larger hooks often require the file, while smaller hooks can be attended to with the diamond grit devices.

Large hooks (1/0 and larger) usually require a file; smaller hooks can probably be attended to with either a diamond grit or a ceramic sharpener. The best of these are impregnated with diamond grit. Ceramic hook sharpeners will work, but generally not as well. For salt water use, however, ceramic sharpeners are recommended because the shafts of diamond grit sharpeners are subject to rusting in this environment.

It's easiest to sharpen a hook before you dress it as a fly. When working, always sharpen away from the point of the hook. If you draw the sharpener down to the point of the hook, you will probably leave a small burr that will keep the point from being sharp. I usually shape a triangular point on trout and small salt water hooks and a diamond-shaped point on large salt water hooks.

Flies

How Do I Get A Fly This Small On My Leader?

If you have difficulty threading your fly to the leader, particularly in low light conditions, these suggestions may help.

Flip Focals are magnifying devices that easily attach to your eyeglasses or polarized glasses and flip down to give you magnification when needed. After you have the fly threaded, merely flip the magnifiers up out of your way or remove them and store them in your vest. Flip Focals come in a variety of diopter powers, so you can choose the one best for your eyesight.

In your vest, carry a flashlight small enough to hold in your teeth or clip to your hat when in use. If the light is waterproof, even better.

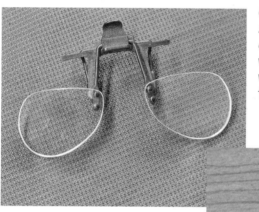

Clip-on magnifiers, which attach to eyeglasses or sunglasses, provide welcome magnification when you're threading flies.

A flashlight with a hat clip allows you to attach the flashlight to the brim or bill of your hat, leaving both hands free to deal with knots, tangles or fly selection.

For small flies, a Threader Fly Box made by C & F Designs Ltd. is invaluable. The box contains small wire threaders that are pushed through the eyes of your flies in preparation for tying the flies on. (Spare threaders in various sizes are also available separately.) You can load the threaders at home in good light and with magnification, if required. Each threader will accommodate a number of flies. To attach the fly to a tippet, simply insert about an inch of the tippet

Small wire fly threaders can be loaded at home in preparation for tying flies on tippet in the field.

through the diamond-shaped hole at the top of the threader and then lift the fly straight up off the wire. As the fly passes over the end of the wire threader, the tippet is sucked into the eye of the fly and you are ready to knot the tippet to the fly. Over the years I have tried a number of other devices advertised for the purpose, but none work as well as this.

The same company makes another, similar, valuable tool. The "3 In 1 Tweezers" is a small pair of plastic tweezers to which a threader and bodkin are attached. The tweezers are handy for picking small flies out of a fly box, the bodkin is useful to clear head cement from the eyes of flies, and the threader is an aid to tying on flies while on the stream. I find I use this tool a lot, particularly for tying on flies with heads of spun deer hair. Such flies are difficult to attach to leaders because the deer hair tends to push the tippet away before it enters the eye of the hook. To mount such flies, I first insert the threader into the eye of the hook and then proceed to put the tippet through the diamond on the threader, making the whole chore much easier.

Any time you tie on a fly in low light conditions, position the fly such that you are looking at it with a background of a single, solid colour—like the dark green of a tree or the overhead sky. A multi-coloured background just adds to your difficulty.

Tweezers and threader

Deer hair fly on threader

Floatants and Desiccants

Most anglers carry some sort of paste floatant in their vests, but those floatants only solve part of the problem of keeping a dry fly floating properly. You should also carry a desiccant to dry off a saturated or fish-mouthed fly. Desiccants come in plastic lidded containers in crystal form. To dry the fly, simply open the lid of the container, insert the fly (still attached to the tippet), hold the lid closed and shake the container. The desiccant crystals will remove water from the fly. Desiccants are invaluable on the stream to recondition sodden flies. They also last a very long time. If the desiccant container as bought does not allow you to insert the fly with ease, pour the desiccant crystals into a plastic 35 mm film container. You now have a wide-mouthed container that will facilitate fly insertion.

Paste floatants should be used sparingly. If the fly's hackles or tail are sticking together after you apply the paste floatant, you've applied too much, which can actually sink the fly. Once the fly has been saturated with water or mouthed by a fish, do not apply more paste floatant without drying the fly first with a desiccant. If you do, you simply seal in the water and the fly will sink.

Paste floatants only solve part of the problem of keeping a dry fly floating. A desiccant reconditions sodden flies.

Insects

Some anglers enjoy capturing and identifying insect specimens. Many insects have common names, but these vary from place to place, and the multiplicity of common names can lead to confusion. For example, what anglers in the Rocky Mountain area call "March Browns" may or may not be the same as what Eastern anglers call "March Browns." The use of scientific taxonomy avoids this potential confusion. This method of naming identifies a particular insect so specifically that you can speak with a person in Budapest about an *Ephemerella enermis* and know that you are both talking about the same critter. Scientific taxonomy gives every insect (or plant for that matter) a name consisting of two parts, comparable to the way we name people. The first part of the scientific name tells the genus, or group, to which the insect belongs. We can compare this to the surname, or family name, such as "Brown." The second part of the scientific name indicates the species, or particular member of the group. This is comparable to the given or Christian name of an individual, such as "William" of "William Brown." The precision of scientific names avoids the potential confusion of common names.

All fly fishers should have a simple working knowledge of entomology, because it is important to know the difference between a mayfly and a caddis fly when selecting flies to match the naturals. But, in my view, scientific specificity is not necessary to success in fly fishing, so don't get scared off by the scientific names some anglers employ. If you do not wish to partake in identifying insects by their scientific names, that's okay. Neither do the fish. I have never talked to a fish, but I will bet if I could, he wouldn't "know" his quarry's Latin and/or Greek name.

Knots

Practice Your Knots

Sound knots are mandatory for successful angling. Most knots are relatively easy to tie, and all are easier to tie if you practice. Practice knots at home until they become second nature. More fish are lost because of poorly tied knots than probably any other single reason. There are enough things that can (and do) go wrong in an angling situation without introducing an avoidable problem. Practice the knots you will use.

Non-Slip Loop Knots For Streamers

Streamers are flies that imitate swimming organisms, such as minnows and leeches. When I am fishing streamers I attach the fly with a loop knot, which allows the streamer to "swim" better than does a hard knot such as a clinch knot. I also use this knot for attaching bonefish flies to a leader. As strong as a clinch knot, the non-slip loop knot allows the fly to swing in the water.

The best loop knot for this purpose is tied as follows:

Step 1. Tie an overhand knot in the tippet.

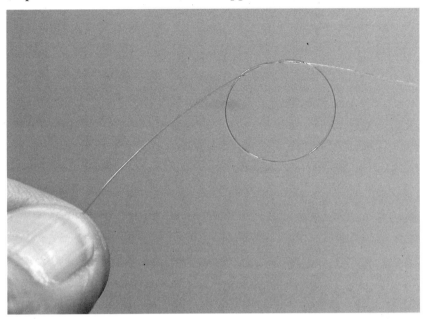

Step 2. Put the tag end of the tippet through the eye of the fly and then through the overhand knot.

Step 3. Let the overhand knot slide down near the eye of the hook, but do not tighten the knot completely. Wrap the tag end of the tippet around the standing line of the tippet 5 or 6 times, working away from the overhand knot.

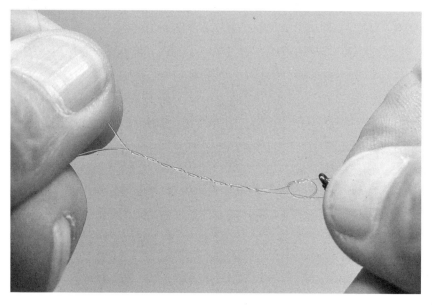

Step 4. Insert the tag end of the tippet through the overhand knot and tighten by pulling on the tag end of the tippet.

Step 5. As the tag end of the tippet tightens, the loop is formed at the point where the overhand knot was sitting.

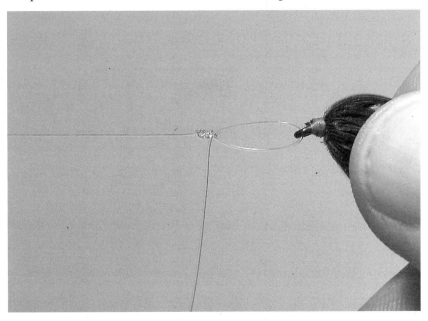

Step 6. Clip off tag end of tippet and knot is finished. The size of the loop is dependent on where the overhand knot is sitting when the knot is tightened.

Homer Rhodes Loop Knot

For attaching a fly to monofilament or fluorocarbon shock tippet, the Homer Rhodes Loop Knot is the preferred connection. Easy to tie and with a relatively small profile, it also allows the fly to swing in the water. This knot is not particularly strong, but that is not terribly important when dealing with shock tippets that are 40#—100# break strength. I would not recommend this knot for attaching streamers to standard leaders, preferring the non-slip loop knot described above.

Step 1. Put a simple overhand knot in the shock tippet, leaving several inches of tag end to work with.

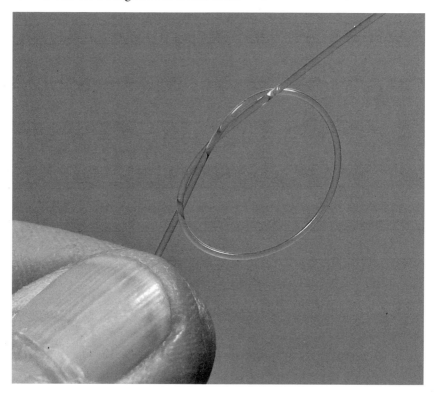

Step 2. Put the tag end of the shock tippet through the eye of the hook and then through the overhand knot. Tighten the overhand knot and allow it to slide down in front of the eye of the hook.

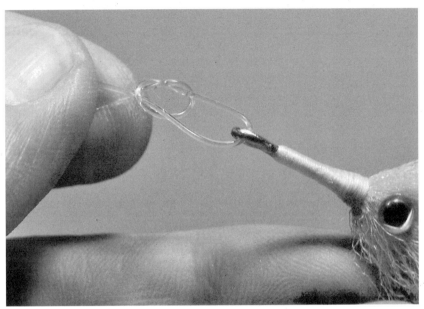

Step 3. Use the tag end to tie another overhand knot, trapping the standing line of the shock tippet inside the second overhand knot.

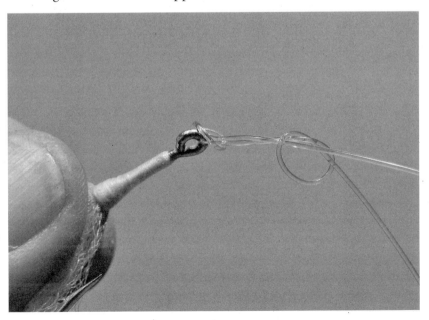

Step 4. Snug up the second overhand knot around the standing line of the shock tippet.

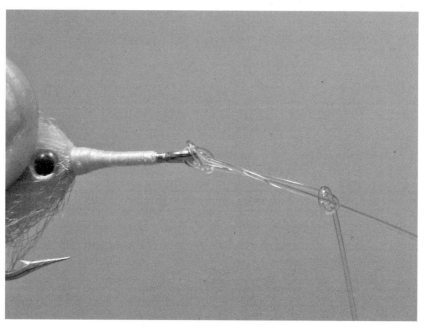

Step 5. Tighten the second overhand knot using pliers, while at the same time keeping a good grip on the fly so it does not jump forward and stick into your hand.

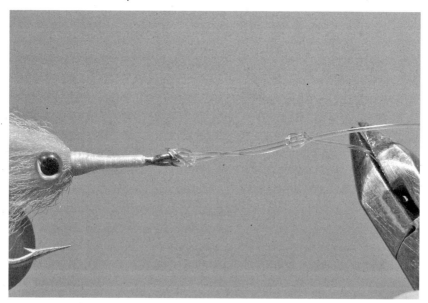

Step 6. When the second overhand knot is tight, hang onto the fly and pull on the standing line of the shock tippet. The two overhand knots will slide together and jam, forming the loop connection. Clip off the tag end and the knot is complete.

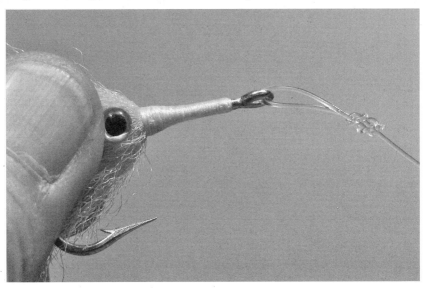

Lines

Mark Your Fly Lines For Weight

When you purchase a fly line, the manufacturer will almost always include a stick-on line designation marker in the package. This sticker is meant to be affixed to the reel or spool to remind you which line is on the reel or spool. I find these generally useless because the adhesive on the back of the sticker will not keep the designator on your reel or spool for long. They get wet and fall apart, or the adhesive ceases to stick and the whole thing wads up inside the reel.

Instead, I mark the line itself a few inches from the tip with a permanent black marking pen. The pen will not damage the line's performance and the mark will eliminate confusion when you have more than one fly line. In the system I have adopted, a wide black band equals 5 and a narrow black band equals 1. Thus, a wide black band alone tells me that the fly line is a #5. A wide black band plus a narrow black band equals a #6, i.e. 5 + 1 = 6. Two wide black bands designate a #10, i.e. 5 + 5 = 10. For line weights lighter than five, I

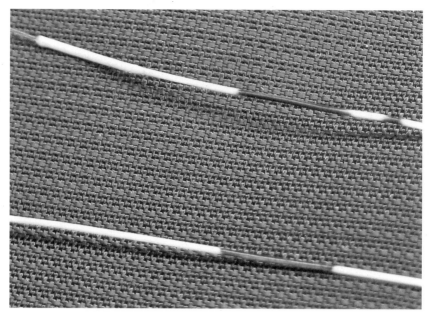

I use a permanent black marking pen to mark my lines' weights using a narrow/wide band code.

put narrow bands on the line in equal number to the line weight. For example, a #3 line will have three narrow black bands on the tip of the line; a #4 line will have four. For sinking tip lines, I put the marks on the floating portion of the line, just past the sinking portion.

I find this system very helpful. If you do not adopt some sort of system, confusion will creep in. The line designator stickers will disappear or become illegible, and there is no way visual inspection alone will tell you which line is a #5 and which is a #6.

Wind Line on Reel Under Tension

Always wind line on a reel under some tension. Hold onto the line with a couple of fingers on your rod hand as you wind. If you don't adopt this habit, you'll be sorry. Tight loops of line will fall inside loose loops and a backlash will occur. If this has happened to you, you already know the frustration. Worse yet, this overlap of line can transmit itself a long distance down inside the reel, even into the backing. Such a backlash will make itself known at a critical time when a big fish is running away at high speed. Over the years I re-spooled any number of reels that evidenced this problem. Seldom did the owners even know it existed.

Always wind line on a reel under some tension to prevent backlash.

Whitlock Zap-A-Gap Splice for Leaders

If I am using a leader substantially longer than my rod, I usually con-
nect the leader to the line using a Zap-A-Gap splice. This splice was
first shown to me by Mike Guinn, an outfitter on the Bow River, who
learned it from Dave Whitlock. This splice will give you the smoothest connection between the line and leader. If you are fishing long
leaders, such as those often employed in lake fishing, at some point
the line/leader connection will be drawn through the guides while
you are fighting the fish. To prevent the connection from hanging up
in the guides, as the traditional knot might, you want the connection
as smooth as possible. This splice does the job beautifully.

You will require:
Zap-A-Gap; Zip Kicker or some other accelerating catalyst for the
adhesive; a pin vise (available at many hobby shops) and a beading
needle, or a 3 In 1 Knot Tool; a small piece of sandpaper; a pair of
forceps; and the leader you wish to install.

To make the splice you can use either a pin vise or the needle portion of a 3 In 1 Tool. If you use a pin vise, first insert a beading needle
into the pin vise, pointed end first, with the eye of the needle protrud-
ing from the vise.

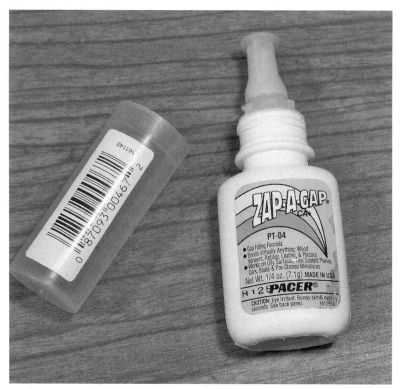

Zap-A-Gap

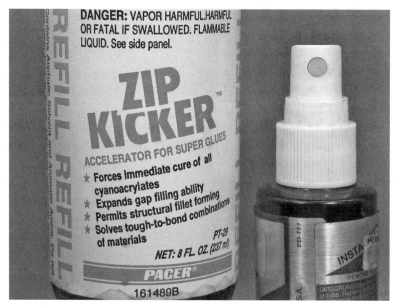

Kicker: an accelerating catalyst for the adhesive.

Pin vise

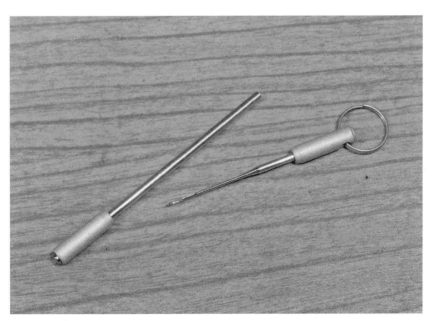

3 In 1 tool open

To make the splice, follow these steps:

Step 1. Insert the eye of the needle into centre core at the end of the fly line and work the needle into the fly line approximately ½ to ¾ of an inch. (If you are using the needle portion of the 3 In 1 Knot Tool, the eye is just behind the point of the needle so you insert the point of the needle into the end of the line.) Push the eye of the needle through the wall of the fly line.

Step 2. Take your leader by the tippet end and insert the tippet into the eye of the needle, pulling about 1 inch of tippet through the eye of the needle.

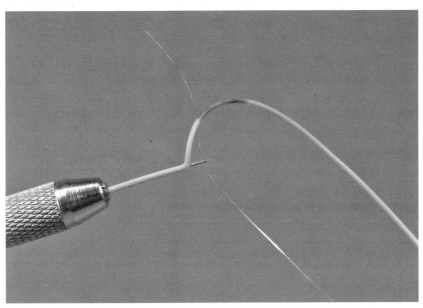

Step 3. Carefully pull the needle out of the inside of the line, drawing the tippet end through the side wall of the line and out of the centre of the fly line.

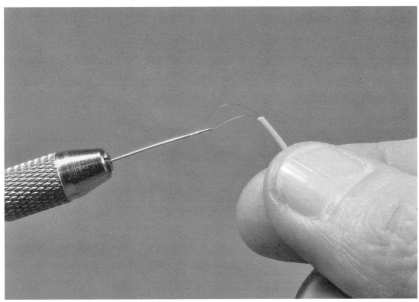

Step 4. Grasp the tippet and pull the entire leader through the fly line until you have all but about ¾ of an inch of leader butt extending from the end of the fly line.

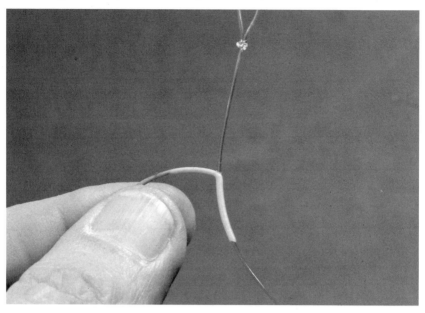

Step 5. Take a small piece of sandpaper and rough up the final ¾ of an inch of the leader butt. This will give the adhesive an "edge" to adhere to.

Step 6. Attach a pair of forceps to the butt end of the leader.

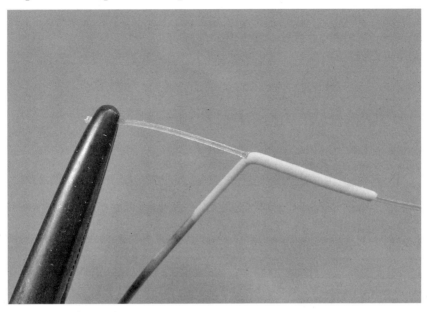

Step 7. Then pull the roughened leader butt through the end of the fly line.

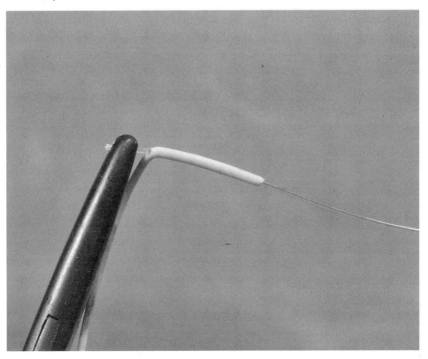

Step 8. Apply a drop of Zap-A-Gap adhesive to the roughened leader butt.

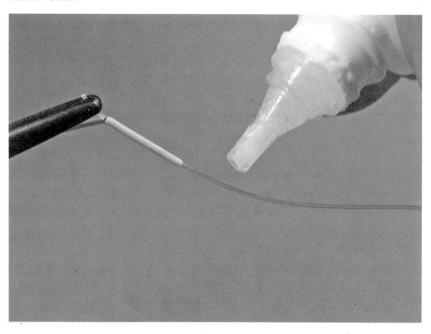

Step 9. Quickly and gently pull back with the forceps, seating the leader butt inside the tip of the fly line.

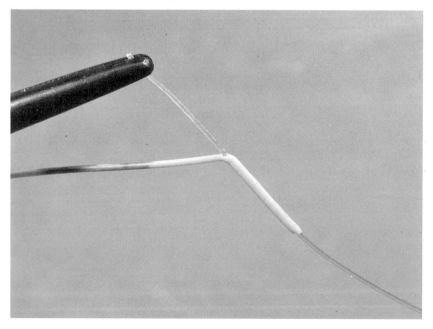

Step 10. Spray the connection with the accelerator to fix the adhesive.

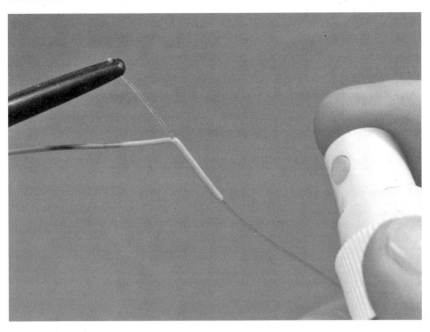

Step 11. Remove the forceps and clip the leader butt as closely as possible to the wall of the fly line.

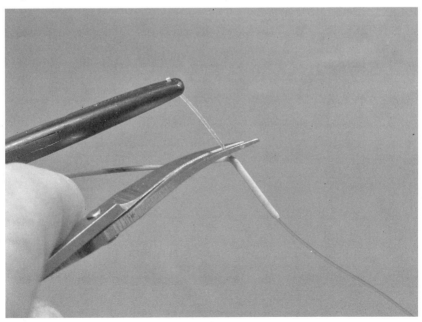

Step 12. Pull on the leader to seat the leader butt inside the fly line and the connection is completed.

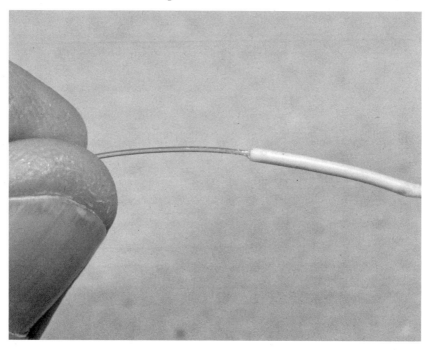

If properly accomplished, this connection will not let go, even under a tremendous amount of pressure. I admit I had some doubts at first, but having now used the connection for years, I'm convinced it will hold. I know it is the smoothest connection that can be constructed and will not hang up in the guides of the rod.

Shock Tippets

As you expand your target species beyond trout, you will find that some species of gamefish require you to employ a shock tippet on your leader. A shock tippet is a short piece of heavy material added at the front of the leader to prevent the fly from being abraded or bitten off the leader. Shock tippets are necessary for northern pike, barracuda, shark, snook, tarpon and trevally, among others—in short, any species that has a lot of sharp teeth or a hard, bony, abrasive mouth. The shock tippet might be wire (for pike, muskie, barracuda or shark) or heavy monofilament or fluorocarbon (tarpon and snook).

Wire shock tippets can be attached to the leader using an Albright knot, as follows:

Step 1. Cut a piece of wire about 10 to 12 inches long and double back one end of the wire to form a loop about an inch long.

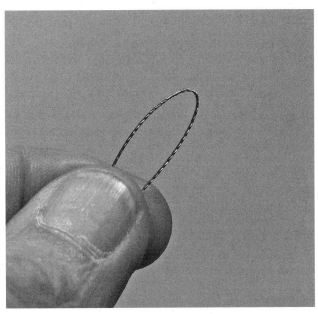

Step 2. Insert the end of the monofilament leader into the wire loop, drawing the monofilament through the loop to give yourself several inches of monofilament to work with.

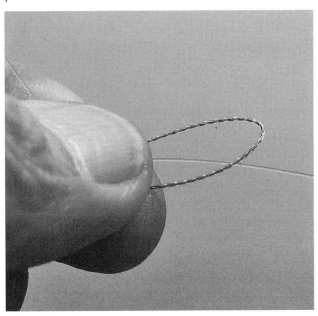

Step 3. Using the tag end of the monofilament, wrap the monofilament over both legs of the wire loop and itself several times, working back toward the open end of the wire loop.

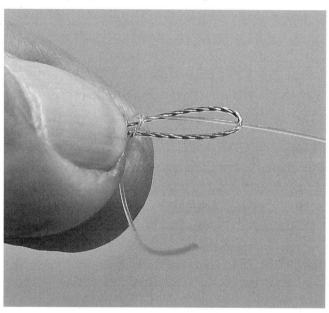

Step 4. Insert the monofilament tag end back through the open end of the wire loop.

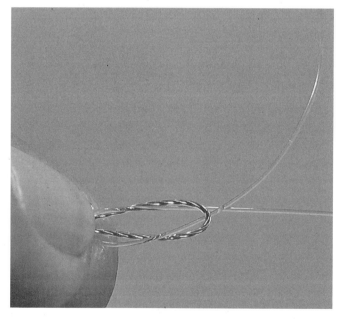

Step 5. Tighten the knot by pulling on both ends of the monofilament. Clip off the tag ends of the monofilament and the wire.

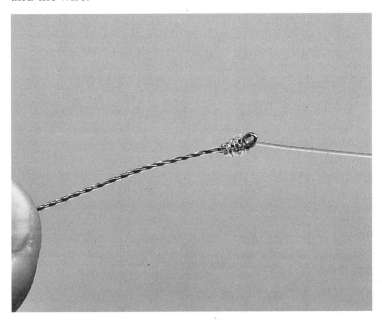

The fly can now be attached to the end of the shock tippet. If you are using nylon coated wire, insert the end of the shock tippet through the eye of the hook, wind the tag end around the standing portion of the shock tippet several times and then flash the knot with a butane lighter. The heat will fuse the nylon and secure the fly. If the tippet wire is limp enough, you might be able to attach the fly using a Homer Rhodes Loop Knot, page 72.

Wire shock tippets are often recommended for pike fishing, but I prefer monofilament or fluorocarbon. I'm convinced from experience that you will get more bites from pike if the shock tippet is transparent. A number of years ago I was pike fishing with a friend and we had one of those rare days when large pike were stacked up in a particular shallow bay in a lake. On any cast we could legitimately anticipate a grab. As the morning progressed, my friend had a number of follows by large pike, but the fish would not bite the fly. I, on the other hand, was experiencing consistent bites. The only difference between his rigging and mine was that his tippet was wire while mine was monofilament. As an experiment, I changed his to monofilament. After that, the number of bites immediately evened out. You will lose some pike to bite-offs using monofilament, but I would rather have a bite and risk the loss than not have the bite at all. A monofilament or fluorocarbon shock tippet can be prepared exactly the same way as the wire shock tippet described above. Simply substitute heavy monofilament or fluorocarbon for the wire in the tying sequence. Once the shock tippet is attached, use the Homer Rhodes Loop Knot, page 72, to attach the fly.

The biggest problem with monofilament and fluorocarbon shock tippets is that these materials have a significant memory (a curl) when taken off a spool. To function properly, the shock tippets must be straightened. You can do this using copper pipe and tapwater. Obtain a copper pipe at the local home renovation or hardware store and cut it to about 14 inches long. Buy two cap fittings for the pipe and epoxy one to one end of the pipe. Keep the second cap for later. Cut your 60#, 80#, and 100# monofilament or fluorocarbon to a suitable length to fit inside the pipe, and continue to add pieces until the whole diameter of the pipe is full of material. Once the pipe is completely packed with the material to be straightened, put the open pipe full of tippets into a tray of water and leave it there, even for several days. At the end of that time, the shock tippets should come out of the pipe looking like uncooked spagetti from a box. It is important the pipe be filled with the tippet material when it is immersed because, as the tippet material absorbs water and becomes pliable, the pieces force each

You can straighten curled shock tippets using copper pipe and tap water.

other to straighten. Once they're straight, let them dry. Use the second cap to seal the pipe so the material does not fall out. The material will stay straight until you need to use it. If you want, you can colour-code the various weights of material. I usually mark the tips of 100# material with a black waterproof marker, the tips of 80# material with blue and the tips of 60# material with red. If you want to speed up the straightening process, put the pipe in hot water and recycle hot water into the tray when the water cools.

From time to time, I have been asked why we use a short section of shock tippet at all—why not just use six to nine feet of the heavy material coming off the end of the fly line? A reasonable question. The answer is that you want the breaking strength of the leader section to be lower than the breaking strength of the backing behind the fly line. If you simply add a long section of heavy monofilament to the front of the line, your backing becomes the weakest point in the system, and things always break first at the weakest point. You could see your expensive fly line swim away behind a large fish.

Don't Just Wind That Leader On The Reel

When you are finished fishing for the day, don't simply wind the leader completely onto the reel because it can be difficult to find the tippet end when you want to restring the rod. If you take the time to push the tippet end through one of the ventilation ports in the side

When you're finished fishing for the day, push the tippet end through one of the reel ventilation ports to ease finding the leader end next time.

of the reel, you will then be able to easily find the leader end the next time you go to rig up the rod.

Casting

Keep Your Rod Tip Down

"Keep your rod tip down" is a refrain most anglers hear repeatedly when fishing in a drift boat or flats skiff with a guide. "Drop your rod tip," "Keep your rod tip low," "Lower your rod tip"—words to this effect are so pervasive that if guides did not speak them, their boats would likely be as quiet as libraries. Guides employ this mantra because fishing with an elevated rod tip is bad practice and poor fishing technique. Why? Because a raised rod tip creates an enormous amount of slack in the line.

Consider the common garden hose with a lawn sprinkler attached. If you want to move the sprinkler from one position on the lawn to another, you have two choices: either walk over, pick up the sprinkler and move it; or pull on the hose. If you choose to pull on the hose,

"Keep your rod tip down" is the mantra of fishing guides everywhere for good reason.

the sprinkler will not move until the hose is straight, that is, until the slack is removed from the hose. A fly at the end of a leader behaves precisely the same way. After you've cast, whether with a dry fly or streamer, make sure your rod tip is pointing down and at the fly and all slack is removed from the line. That way, you have direct contact with the fly and can set the hook by pulling on a straight line.

If you think I am belabouring this, it's because this concept is apparently so misunderstood or foreign to many anglers. For the sake of science and guide sanity, let's perform the following experiment:

Grab a rod and reel, go outside on the lawn and string the rod. Pull about 40 feet of line through the tip guide, lay the line on the lawn, and then back up with the rod until the line lies straight away on the ground, with no slack between the reel and the tip end of the line. At this point, back up another couple of steps, pointing the rod tip down at the line, with the rod tip only a couple of inches from the ground. Stop for a moment and confirm that the rod tip is pointed low to the ground and at the straight line extended on the lawn. From this position, rotate your wrist slowly upwards to raise the rod tip to about 45 to 50 degrees, then stop. Now slowly rotate your wrist downward, returning the rod tip to its original position only a couple of inches from the ground.

As the rod tip comes down you will notice that miraculously you have several feet of slack line accumulating under the rod tip, none of which was there before the rod tip was raised. That slack line was created by lifting of the rod tip. "So what?" you say. Well, having performed this little exercise, you should now know that every time you raise the rod tip when fishing, you are introducing slack into an otherwise straight line. In order to set the hook when a fish grabs, you have to make the fly move. Remember the sprinkler? You cannot make the fly move until you remove the slack from the line. Most often, the fish will grab the fly and spit it out before you can remove the slack you have introduced into the line. The raised rod tip causes you to miss strikes. The higher the rod tip when fishing, the more slack is created and the greater the difficulty in setting the hook. This is why guides appear to have such a limited vocabulary.

Similarly, if you begin the next cast with a high rod tip, you are starting with a lot of slack in the line, and that slack has to be removed before the back cast will straighten. Most casters simply cannot do it, so to compensate for the slack, the rod begins to move in wide strokes, creating huge loops and inefficient casts. The raised rod tip has thus set up a problem the caster doesn't understand. The raised rod problem also often leads to excessive false casting as the caster tries to rid himself of all the slack. Before a cast, the line must be straight, and the line cannot be straight unless the rod tip is low and pointing along the line. I once fished with a really extraordinarily talented guide who advised me to put the rod tip slightly into the water when retrieving a fly for bonefish. The next cast was made from that starting position, so the line was straight at the outset and false casting kept to a minimum.

Some Thoughts on Casting

The skill of fly casting is virtually impossible to learn from a book. In this way it is much like learning to swim. If you want to learn to swim, you really have to get into the water, preferably with a qualified instructor. Having said this, there are three very basic casting concepts that may be helpful:

1. The fly line always goes where the rod tip goes. The line's movement always mimics the rod tip's movement. If you want to prove this to yourself, string up a rod and pull about 10 feet of line through the tip guide. Grasp the rod handle and roll the rod tip in large, lazy circles above the floor or grass. The line will rotate in large, lazy circles following the rod tip. The fly line always goes where the rod tip goes.

The corollary is equally important. The rod tip always determines where the line goes. Sounds simple, and it is, but the concept is crucial to your casting. For example, if you want to make the fly line go in a straight line, the rod tip must move in a straight line. If the rod tip's trajectory is curved, the fly line's will likewise curve. Many of us were taught about casting by reference to the clock face. Remember the old saw from *A River Runs Through It?* "It [fly casting] is an art that is performed on a four-count rhythm between ten and two o'clock." Well, like a lot of old saws, this one is incorrect, but so oft repeated that people assume it's true. A rod tip moving from 10 to two o'clock describes a curved, not a straight, path. The line, mimicking the tip's movement, will do the same. Your cast can therefore not be straight. You can prove this as well. Put a rod tip section flat on the floor pointing to 10 o'clock. Keeping the ferrule stationary as a fulcrum, slowly rotate the tip section to the two o'clock position. Watch the tip guide on the rod section and you will see that its course is curved.

If you are going to cast by the clock, discard the "10 to two" concept and adopt an "11 to one" approach. Reverting to the last experiment and placing the tip section on the floor, now point the rod tip to 11 o'clock and rotate it slowly to the one o'clock position. You will see the tip guide more closely draw a straight path, which will impart a straight course to the fly line. The same will be true from 12 to two, or from 10 to 12, simply shifting between a high back/low forward and a low back/high forward cast.

In the final analysis, the shorter movement of a rod tip through two hours on the clock face will make the line straighter and tighten up the loop of line as it travels through the air.

In practical terms, this concept is easily seen in the field. If you drop your back cast tip too far back (past one o'clock), the inertia of the line will be directed back and downward, sending the line curving back and down to slap the water behind you. Similarly, if you drop the tip of the rod too far past eleven o'clock on the forward cast, the line will travel down and forward, slapping the water in front.

Another very similar casting error is directly related to this discussion. I refer to the caster who, rather than take the hand straight back to a stop on the back cast and straight forward again for the forward cast (as when driving in a nail with a hammer), instead pivots the hand and wrist "open" on the back stroke and then pivots the hand and wrist "closed" on the forward stroke (as you might do with a racquet). This movement also causes the rod tip to take a curved path (albeit in a different plane), with the result that the line travels in a curve, often tying some ingenious knots in the process. This habit takes some real discipline and determination to correct.

Certainly some fishing situations call for an open loop and curved line movement, but in most situations a straight line approach is better. The important thing is to understand the cause of open loops and to be capable of throwing them when you want to, not because you've committed to the erroneous 10 to two "rule."

2. Slack line cannot be cast. Every cast should be started by lowering the rod tip, removing the slack line with your line hand, and then commencing the cast with a straight line. If the rod tip is high when you begin the cast (and the line thus slack), you will tend to move the rod too far back on the back cast in an effort to straighten the line. That action causes the rod tip's course to curve, and the line to follow the rod tip in a similarly curved fashion. Your cast is ruined—a bad beginning having rendered a bad ending. (For further explanation, refer to previous section "Keep Your Rod Tip Down.")

3. The reel should lead every cast and the power should be applied at the end of the stroke. When you make a cast, forward or back, the first piece of the outfit to move is the reel. At the start of a back cast, the hand should move back without any rotation and the reel should move back ahead of the rod tip. After a short movement, perhaps 12 inches, the wrist is then accelerated and flipped such that the rod tip catches up to and passes the reel. After this acceleration occurs, the rod should be stopped. The acceleration of the rod tip by the wrist flip at the end of the stroke, coupled with the ensuing stop, creates the casting loop and imparts inertia to the line so it will climb up behind you and straighten. Only after the line has become straight behind you (or virtually so) should you reverse the energy and commence the forward cast. If you do not wait for the line to become straight, you are then attempting to cast slack line.

The forward stroke is the opposite image of the back cast. First the hand moves forward, with the reel leading the rod tip. After pushing the hand forward about 12 inches, the wrist is then accelerated, flipping the rod tip forward such that it catches up to the reel and passes it as the rod is stopped. Stopping the rod at the 11 o'clock position allows the loop to form and roll off the rod tip, sending the line forward to become straight in front.

Notice that, in both the back and forward cast, the reel should lead the rod tip, reserving the application of power until the end of the stroke. The application of power and the stopping of the rod tip creates the loop. If you apply power too early in the stroke, the rod tip will lead the reel and gravity will drive the top of the loop beneath the bottom of the loop before the line straightens. This usually runs the line into itself and ties knots in it or the leader. You end up casting an undesirable tailing loop.

Practice Your Casting

As peculiar as it might sound, casting is perhaps the most neglected aspect of the sport by most anglers. As a case in point, for a number of years we offered "intermediate level" fly fishing schools through the shop. Two formats were offered: a dry land "casting improvement" session of about two hours; and a day "on the water" with an instructor. The "on the water" schools were very popular, but the "casting improvement" sessions left the instructor about as much to do as the famous Maytag repairman. In an interesting twist, the "on the water" instructors would often opine afterward that almost all of that day's students would have profited more from a casting improvement session than they had from the day on the river.

Casting is perhaps the most important single aspect of the sport and should be practiced often in order to "groove" the cast. And do not be deceived into thinking you are practicing your casting when you are out fishing. Golfers and tennis players, who practice consistently, do not confuse practice with playing the game. Make a regular habit of *practicing*. Go to a park or pond near your home. One caveat, however. Be prepared for some passerby to shout, "Are you catching any?" It happens every time and the shouter invariably thinks his wisecrack the height of hilarity.

Always use a target when practicing—a hula hoop, hat, bucket, base on a ball diamond or whatever. Using a target will better hone your accuracy than randomly throwing line. Practice casting different loop shapes such that you can throw an open loop when one might be called for in the field. Make a habit of watching your loops as you cast. Knowing how they behave will help you to correct casting errors.

Practice changing the attitude of the rod; throw side arm and backhand casts as part of your practice routine. Not all fishing situations are conducive to the typical overhead cast, and you should be able to drop into a side arm cast when delivering a fly under an overhanging obstruction. Practice delivering the fly on the back cast too. Many fishing situations are better served with a backhand delivery, but too few anglers ever consider it.

For greatest effect, keep your practice sessions short. A casting session of longer than about 30 minutes is probably not advisable. In longer sessions you'll get fatigued—whether you realize it or not—and fatigue leads to casting errors. For better results, practice more often, not longer.

Practice casting in conditions similar to those you will most commonly encounter when fishing. I once talked to a would-be tarpon fisherman about his casting practice. He assured me he had been practicing, but it turned out he'd done so on calm days, and it stood him in poor stead when he actually was faced with the winds typical of salt water flats fishing.

Do not fall into the common trap of simply trying to cast long lines in your sessions. Long casts might have a place in fishing, but that place is small indeed. Short casts made under control and with accuracy are more important. And they are easier to control, particularly when drag is a problem. In the field, your aim should be never to make a long cast when a short cast will do the job. That means planning your approach so a short cast will work. When trout fishing, the really good anglers catch most of their fish with relatively short casts. Inexperienced fishers, on the other hand, seem to have an obsession with making a long cast. Watch them (and some experienced fishers too) try out a new rod. You'll notice they generally want to see how far the rod will cast the fly. This is a bit like judging an automobile's performance by testing how fast it will go from zero to sixty. Any car will exceed the speed limit, so what's the point? In fly fishing you're better off learning to make an accurate short cast. Leave the long casts in the parking lot.

Most trout anglers false cast far too much. The purpose of false casting is to lengthen line and also to dry the fly off by flicking it in the air. But continuous false casting does little good in either regard—it does nothing but waste time. The fish cannot grab the fly when it's in the air; you'll have better luck with the fly on the water more of the time. Any cast can be made with two cycles: one back cast, one forward cast, a second back cast and then a delivery cast. Practice this technique and you will spend more time actually fishing the fly instead of throwing it around.

Reach Mends

In presenting flies to trout, fishers often use the tactic of "dead drift." That is, they try to get the fly to float as though it were not attached to anything—just the way natural insects drift in current. The problem is, your fly *is* attached to something, your leader and line, which in turn lie on top of water running at different speeds at various points between the stream's banks. Any portion of line that lies in faster water than that where the fly is riding, will "belly" downstream and drag the fly, skating it along the surface in an unnatural way. To alleviate the problem, you can use "mends" in the line. A mend is simply a repositioning of the fly line on the water to introduce some slack in the line and delay the onset of drag. Some "on the water" mends can achieve this, but are usually inefficient and often move the fly. Instead of mending on the water, put the mend into the line while it's still in the air. To accomplish such a "reach mend," the fisher repositions the rod after making the forward power stoke of the cast, but before the line lands on the surface of the water.

Reach mends are much more efficient than on-the-water mends. Learn and practice the technique and you will find the problem of drag considerably diminished. If you do not know how to perform reach mends, get professional advice from your tackle dealer. They are absolutely "must know" techniques.

Two Fly Rigs

A very popular fishing technique is the two fly rig. What you do is affix two flies to the leader, which are then fished simultaneously. You can rig this several ways. One way is to tie a fly to the end of the leader and affix the second fly, the dropper, off a short piece of leader material tied on up the leader. If both are sinking flies, you place a weight between the two flies. You can also effect a two fly rig by attaching two droppers up the leader and putting the weight at the bottom of the leader. A third method is to tie a fly on at the end of the leader, then attach another piece of tippet material to the eye of the first fly, and attach the second fly to that piece of tippet material. I prefer the latter because, the two flies being in straighter line with each other, this rig is the least likely to tangle during casting.

Many people use two sinking flies, with a strike indicator also attached to the leader—a double nymph rig, if you will. The two fly rig might also employ one sinking fly at the bottom with a floating fly up the leader. In this set up, the floating fly can be taken by the fish as a primary fly, or it might act as a strike indicator for the sinking fly below. This floating fly/sinking fly rig is often referred to as a "hopper/dropper" rig because large grasshopper imitations are often used for the floating fly. Likewise, both flies can be floating, known as a double hopper rig; or both can be streamers—a double streamer rig.

All these methods can be effective, but tangling is always a concern when casting two fly rigs. To reduce this possibility, open your casting loop. Another problem is that the fish takes only one fly, leaving the second to wave around and get snagged on things like landing nets, the belly of the hooked fish or, when the fish is landed, nearby guides or anglers.

In some jurisdictions, like British Columbia, it is illegal to use more than one fly at a time. Check regulations where you are fishing to confirm that two fly rigs are allowed.

Fighting a Fish

When a fish takes a fly, the first thing you do is set the hook. You do this by removing any slack line, that is, by making the line straight from your line hand to the fly. Once the hook is set, you need to clear any loose line, by which I mean make the line straight between the fish and the reel. Usually a hooked fish will move away from the pressure, and in doing so, will take away most or all of the slack line. If the fish does not move away a distance sufficient to take up all the slack, wind the balance onto the reel so the line is now straight from reel to fish. If the fish then runs, pull your hand away from the reel and let the fish go, pulling line off the reel as it can. When you can recover line, do so, but be ready at any moment to remove your hand from the reel and let the fish take more line. Never attempt to stop a fish by holding onto the line or reel handle. Never attempt to play a fish by stripping line in by hand. If you do, the loose line now at your feet will certainly foul on something, tangle the line and break the leader as soon as the fish starts its next run. If a fish runs toward you when hooked, you might be called upon to strip in line by hand to keep the connection tight, but then take extreme care to once again clear the line when the fish turns away. Simple so far.

While all of this is going on, what do you do with the rod? Most people would tell you to keep the rod tip up. Angling is, in fact, a solitary pursuit until you hook a fish, at which time it becomes a gregarious activity, with everyone within earshot of your "screaming" reel suddenly coming over to counsel you as to how to play the fish. And they always tell you to "keep your rod tip up." Well, I hate to be the one to break the news, but that advice is wrong. Keeping the rod tip up will do nothing to tire the fish. A fly rod is a poor lifting tool, and upwards pressure with the rod has little effect.

If you are not convinced, try this exercise. Get a friend to assist. Grab a rod and reel, take them outside where you have plenty of room, and string the rod. Pull the leader and about fifteen or twenty feet of line out of the rod tip and get your assistant to walk away with the leader. Your assistant should then securely wrap the leader around his or her hand and extend the hand toward you as if wanting to shake hands. Now, think about how a fish swims. Virtually all gamefish swim by swaying their tails from side to side. Understanding this, your assistant mimics that action by gently moving the extended hand from side to side, wiggling like a swimming fish. While your assistant is doing this, you tighten up the line and raise the rod tip such that it is in the "keep the rod tip up" position. Do not yank on the rod, just hold it up and bent. Now, ask your assistant if he or she can feel any pressure exerted by the rod. The honest answer will be "No, not particularly." Ask your assistant to continue the swimming action, and gently but firmly pull the rod tip from the upwards attitude to a side position. Ask again. The honest answer now will be "Yes, definitely." The difference between keeping the rod tip up and keeping it bent in an attitude that inhibits swimming motion is monumental. If you still don't believe it, switch places with your assistant, and you be the fish.

The moral is that when fighting a fish, you should not keep the rod tip up, but keep it bent. Moreover, switching the attitude of the bent rod from side to side will wear a fish out quickly. It's the equivalent of pushing sideways on the shoulder of someone running straight down a track. In fact, the sideways energy will probably cause him or her to fall completely off the track. Upward pressure on a fly rod does nothing to interfere with the fish's swimming motion, so, while it might get bored, it won't get tired.

Boats

Boats and Other Fishing Platforms

Anglers love boats. On larger western rivers, boats of various descriptions have long been used as fishing platforms and a means of access to parts of rivers not easily accessed by foot. Riverboats, driftboats, guide boats, river guide boats, dories, prams, McKenzie boats, Rogue River boats, rafts, inflatables—whatever they're called, virtually all are designed to be rowed upstream against the current by someone sitting in the middle of the boat, looking downstream. The anglers sit at each end, casting as the boat drifts downstream. It is an effective fishing platform, and taking a float trip can be a very enjoyable way to spend a day. On larger rivers, virtually every guide has one of these boats and employs it to ply his or her trade. The merits and demerits of each are widely, and sometimes hotly, debated. I have fished from and rowed a wide variety of craft. In the final analysis, I paraphrase an old university professor of mine: "All men think their dogs are beautiful, but we have seen some men's dogs." I believe that choosing any particular craft is a compromise, in that none will do all things perfectly. Hard-sided boats, whether made of fibreglass or aluminum, usually row well and have lots of creature comfort room, but can be ill-suited to fast, shallow, rock-infested rivers with the potential for frequent collisions. In such rivers, a self-baling inflatable raft might be preferred, though these soft-sided boats often do not have a great deal of room for gear. If you are thinking of getting a fishing boat, I suggest you do serious investigation and some "mean considerin'" before jumping in (as it were). Your choices are many, so choose based on which craft best suits what you want to do most often.

Once you have your craft, get some advice on how to row it, then practice your rowing on benign waters before you launch onto technically difficult streams. If you've never rowed one of these boats, you'll quickly discover it's not as easy as an experienced oarsman makes it appear. Even before you get the boat wet, I'd suggest you read Neale Streeks's exceptional book *Drift Boat Strategies*.

A couple of other fishing platforms deserve mention—belly boats and pontoon boats. Belly boats have been around for decades; pontoon boats are a relatively recent innovation. A belly boat is essentially a truck tire inner tube with a covering attached whereby the user can sit in the middle of the inner tube suspended by a seat, float around, and fish. They are effective platforms, but designed exclusively for still water use and should only be used in still waters. In a belly boat you are sitting navel deep in the water, with your legs dangling below the water's surface. As a consequence, a belly boat is dangerous in moving water, where your legs could get tangled in some sunken obstruction.

A pontoon boat is a pair of inflatable bladders (that look like large hot dogs) joined together by a frame that keeps the two bladders parallel to each other. The user sits up out of the water between the pontoons, with just the feet and lower legs dangling in the water. In the original design, the user was expected to move the craft using swim fins. When they first appeared, I thought they would be an alternative fishing platform to compete with belly boats, being relatively small and lightweight, inexpensive, and easy to transport. Moreover, they apparently would have the potential for safe use in moving waters because the user could lift his feet and legs out of the water at will—

impossible in a belly boat. I was mistaken. Rather than paring down the new pontoon boat conception to compete with belly boats, the manufacturers went the opposite direction, tricking out pontoon boats like one-man drift boats, with rowing frames, oars and gear decks. This move was apparently well received by the angling public, judging by the numbers of pontoon boats now seen on western waters, both still and moving.

I think lots of anglers bought pontoon boats thinking they could have the benefits of a drift boat at a fraction of the cost, and would have access to rivers heretofore accessible only to driftboats. In that, perhaps they were mistaken. In my experience, pontoon boats are excellent still water fishing platforms, but leave a lot to be desired on moving water. As any experienced guide will tell you, boat placement can be critical to angling success. The downfall of the pontoon boat on moving water is that the user cannot attend to boat placement and casting at the same time. In a one-person craft, you can fish or you can row—you can't do both at once. As the current gets more technically demanding, more time and attention must be paid to safe navigation, with a consequent reduction of fishing time. If you use a pontoon boat simply to convey you to places where you intend to fish on your feet, that will work. If you expect a pontoon boat to avail you the advantages of a driftboat or raft, you may be disappointed.

Boat Plugs

If you do use a boat, always carry extra boat plugs. Never buy them one at a time. They are constantly getting lost, and without a plug, you don't have a boat—you have a submarine. Never take the plug out of a boat and set it on a vehicle's bumper or fender or on the trailer. You'll pull away from the take-out before you remember you put it there, and when you do remember, it won't be there any longer. Carry spares.

Carry spare boat plugs: they're always getting lost. No plug, no boat.

Carry a Camera

I consider a camera an essential piece of my fishing tackle. Many people find toting a camera cumbersome, but I would rather carry one than be without. I use mine all the time and find great satisfaction in the pursuit of good photographs when I am afield. In fact, some of my closest angling friends are amused when I become more excited about a group of tall white bog orchids found along the stream than a rising fish. I also carry a tripod, considering it a necessity, not an accessory. If you carry a camera, take precautions to keep it from getting wet. Expensive cameras dropped into water are nothing more than expensive paperweights. I carry mine in a small waterproof case made by Pelican Products of Torrance, California (www.pelican.com). Such cases are not expensive and are very worthwhile. You might even consider purchasing a waterproof camera. I have used a digital camera for several years and I'm consistently amazed by the results. If you are shooting digital and intend to enlarge your pictures, set the camera for the highest resolution. It will gobble more memory, but the superior results are worth it. I also carry a spare battery and make a point of keeping it charged. If you don't carry a camera, there will be times you'll wish you had.

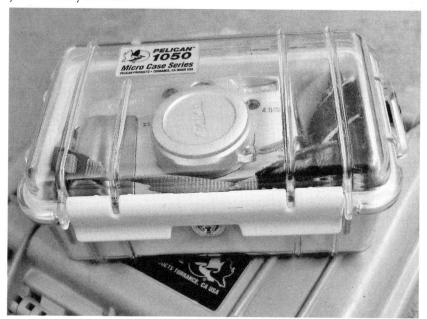

A waterproof case is invaluable for keeping expensive cameras from becoming expensive paperweights.

Keep a Fishing Diary

Many anglers seem to want to trust memory, eschewing the diary, but they will find memory is fleeting. If you have a particularly wonderful day fishing green drakes on a favourite stream, some notes made then will better assist your timely return in future years. If you find a new piece of water, make some notes about how you got there so you can get back. A diary will also help you make predictions about anticipated hatches on diverse streams at various times. If you do not keep a diary now, you will someday wish you had. I keep my diary on the computer because the search feature "Find" in the word processing program is a real help when I'm looking for particular information.

What You Want: Useful Gadgets and Gizmos

If you are fond of gadgets and gizmos, fly fishing provides fertile ground for your predilection. Tour any fly shop or pick up any catalogue and you will see hundreds of things available with, no doubt, more on the way each passing day. It's said that "necessity is the mother of invention." That may be so, but having seen some of the inventions offered for sale, it seems the mother of invention had more children than she could handle. Some of the available gadgets are wonderful; lots are useless (or practically so), just as in every other sport. You will have to make up your own mind about the utility of individual products. What follows is an elucidation of products I have used and think are worthwhile. By way of disclaimer, I was not remunerated in any way by any manufacturer of products shown here, nor was I given samples. Further, I have no proprietary interest in any of the businesses that make or market these products. I endorse them simply because I have found the items meritorious.

Aquaseal and UV Wader Repair

Aquaseal is perfect for repairing almost any wader, whether neoprene, nylon or breathable. This urethane adhesive is easy to use and very effective. It has a cure time of twenty-four to thirty-six hours, but that can be shortened to about two hours by mixing the Aquaseal with Cotol 240 accelerator.

When using these products, work in a well ventilated area and do not use near heat or open flames. Aquaseal is quite viscous, but the Cotol will thin it considerably. Mix the Aquaseal and Cotol in an empty film canister, stirring it with a small Popsicle stick or bamboo

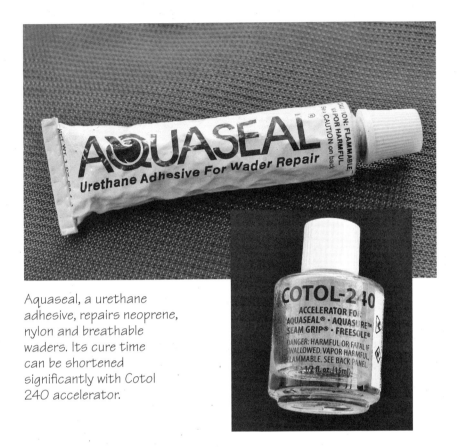

Aquaseal, a urethane adhesive, repairs neoprene, nylon and breathable waders. Its cure time can be shortened significantly with Cotol 240 accelerator.

skewer. The stir stick can also be used as an applicator. The proper working viscosity is a little bit thinner than liquid honey.

Before applying the adhesive, clean the area around the puncture and apply a piece of duct tape as a backing inside the waders so the adhesive will not infiltrate the wader. If you have an "L" shaped tear in the wader material, apply the duct tape to hold the torn edges of the wader material in place. When ready, simply put a bead of the Aquaseal/Cotol mixture on the torn or punctured material and set it aside to cure. Make sure the surface on which you set the waders is flat and level, to prevent the mixture from running.

Aquaseal is packaged in a tube that resembles toothpaste. When new, the end of the tube under the screw cap is sealed with an aluminum foil. You must penetrate the foil to allow the adhesive to get out of the tube. However, once you have opened the tube and used the adhesive, do not simply replace the cap and put the tube on the shelf. The adhesive in the tube will oxidize over time, and the whole tube may become solid before you use it again. To avoid this eventuality after first use, carefully wipe any adhesive from the screw top, put on the cap, then store the tube in the freezer compartment of your refrigerator or in the deep freeze. The cold will prevent the adhesive from oxidizing. When you need to use the adhesive again, remove the tube from the freezer and put it into a cup of hot water for a minute or two. It will be thawed and ready to use. Repeat the procedure after each use, returning it to the freezer until the next time it is needed.

Another good product for repairing waders is UV Wader Repair, made by Loon Outdoors of Boise, Idaho (www.loonoutdoors.com). After backing up the puncture with duct tape on the inside of the waders, simply sqeeze the UV Wader Repair on the puncture in a shaded place, then expose it to sunlight. The ultraviolet rays fix the adhesive. This product can be applied to wet or dry waders.

Inverted Floatant Holders

One of the best "danglies" for a fishing vest is an inverted floatant holder that clips onto your vest and holds your paste floatant container open-end down. Gravity pushes the floatant into the dispenser end, allowing you to use all of the floatant before discarding the container. If you simply tuck the container right side up in your vest pocket, you will never be able to extract all the floatant material. Before these inverted holders were invented, the fly fishing world was strewn with partially full floatant containers. On cold days, it can be hard to release paste floatant from the container because the paste becomes too viscous. On such days, consider attaching the clip of the floatant holder to your shirt pocket flap, tucking the container inside your pocket. Your body heat will usually warm the floatant enough to allow better flow from the dispenser.

Orvis Magnetic Net Release

I use a net when trout fishing and I recommend nets for quick, efficient handling of fish. I particularly like the "catch and release" style of landing nets, with their shallower net bag. When walking in the bush with my net, I tuck the net bag into the back of my wading belt to stop it swinging and getting caught in limbs and bushes.

When the Orvis magnetic net release first appeared on the market, Jim McLennan, my then business partner, and I had a good laugh about it, speculating it would be as useful as a solar-powered pith

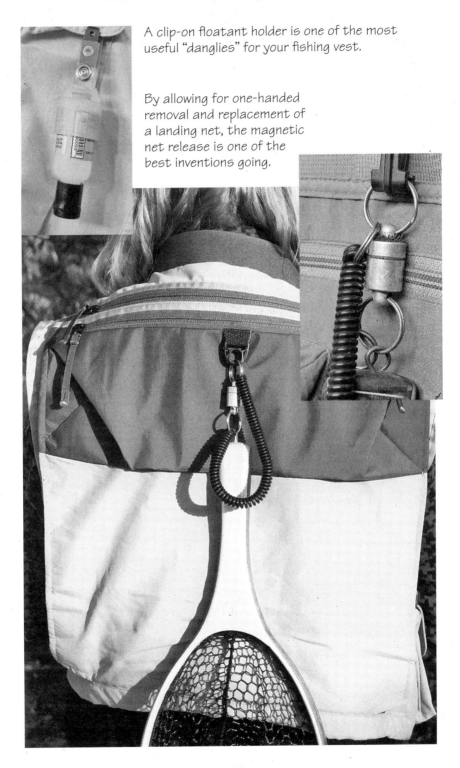

A clip-on floatant holder is one of the most useful "danglies" for your fishing vest.

By allowing for one-handed removal and replacement of a landing net, the magnetic net release is one of the best inventions going.

helmet. On trying it, however, Jim proclaimed it the greatest gadget he had ever used. And I agree. Until its arrival, there was no net release available that allowed for one-handed removal and replacement of a landing net. This one does. You simply attach one of the magnets to the net handle and the other to the "D" ring on the back of your vest. The magnet is strong enough to hold the net up on the back of the vest, but will release when you give the net a sharp tug. After you have used the net, you re-affix it by bringing the magnets into close proximity. The net literally snaps back into place. All other net releases on the market require two hands to reattach your net. The net release also comes with a safety cord that joins the net to the "D" ring on the vest and keeps the net from drifting away if dropped in the water.

The Ketchum Release Tool

Around for several years now, the Ketchum Release tool, made by Waterworks Lamson (www.waterworks-lamson.com), has attracted a large and loyal following. Designed to quickly remove a hook from the mouth of a fish, the end of the tool has a channel of plastic that slips onto the leader. Once on the leader, all you do is slide the tool down the leader to the hook and push. The tool causes the hook to

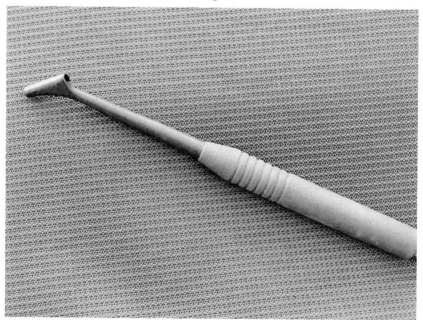

The Ketchum Release tool is designed to quickly remove a hook from the mouth of a fish.

back out of the mouth and get trapped in the channel. This tool will even remove a hook without your having to touch the fish. I know several professional guides that swear by and use it constantly.

The Fly Trap

The same people who brought us the Ketchum Release Tool also make the Fly Trap, which functions as a receptacle for the flies you remove from your leader after use. Having tried it once, I immediately became a big fan and now use it all the time. Traditionally, fly fishers have used fleece patches for this purpose, but they border on useless, particularly for barbless flies. When a hand, fly line, branch or any number of other items sweep against a fleece patch, the flies you've placed there are knocked off and lost. A sodden fly, stuck on a fleece patch, gets mangled and misshapen and won't dry properly. And if you put a fly away wet, the hook rusts, destroying the fly and causing all other

The Fly Trap houses flies you remove from your leader after use, keeping them secure until they're dry.

hooks in the box to rust as well. The Fly Trap solves all these problems. When you want to change flies, simply cut the used fly off the leader, open the Fly Trap door, and secure the fly in the foam ridges inside. Close the lid and the fly is secure. The ventilation ports on each end of the Fly Trap allows the flies inside to dry during the day, so you can return them safely to their fly boxes that evening or next day. I estimate that I save the price of the Fly Trap every day astream by hanging onto flies I used to lose from a fleece patch. A tremendous invention.

Neoprene Reel Pouches

Most modern fly reels are made with an external rim to allow the user to palm the rim for more drag. If the external rim is banged and thus bent, it may start to bind the reel frame, and the reel is essentially ruined. I highly recommend neoprene reel pouches to protect your reels. The spongy material protects the reel from damage caused by being bounced around. More important, the neoprene pouch can be fitted on a reel already mounted on a rod—an advantage over the standard zip-close pouches supplied by many reel manufacturers. This feature is particularly handy in a boat underway to a fishing venue, when your reel needs protection from jostling against the boat's hull. It is interesting to note that almost every manufacturer of high-end reels now supplies this type of case with a new reel. Take the precaution of using the neoprene reel cozy. Most experienced fly fishers do.

The 3 In 1 Tool

The 3 In 1 Tool is a handy device that assists with a number of chores. The tool comprises two parts—a needle and a tube—which fit together by inserting the needle into the tube and pushing them together. The needle end can be used to clear head cement from the eyes of hooks and to tie needle knots for attaching leaders to fly lines. The needle has an eye that makes the tool perfect for installing a Whitlock Zap-A-Gap Splice (page 77) on any fly line. The tube section is useful for tying nail knots. A small magnet in the closed end of the tube is handy for picking out small flies from a fly box. I've carried one for several years.

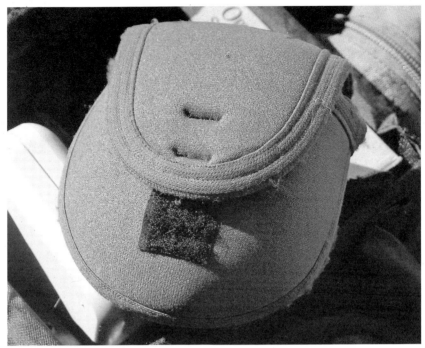

Neoprene reel pouches can be fitted on a reel already mounted on a rod, an advantage over standard zip-close pouches supplied by reel manufacturers.

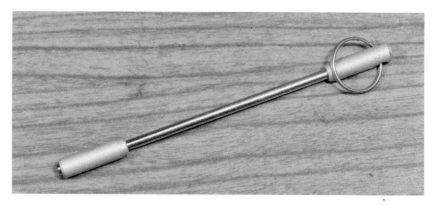

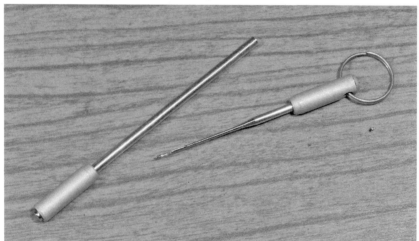

The 3 In 1 Tool is a versatile device that comprises a needle and a tube. A magnet in the tube end is useful too.

Stretcher Box

For pike or tarpon fishing, a worthwhile accessory is a stretcher box. The box is set up with a series of bungee cord loops at one end and opposite slots at the other. The flies, attached to shock tippets, are slotted into the bungee cord loops, then stretched to fit the shock tippet/class tippet connection knot in the opposite slot, keeping the shock tippets under tension and straight.

A stretcher box, which accommodates several flies previously tied on leaders, acts like a magazine for a rifle, holding the "ammunition" that might be required.

The class tippet portion of the leader is wound up and kept together with a small piece of twist tie until the fly is needed. This particular stretcher box will accommodate ten flies on leaders; others might accommodate more. Filled with flies at the beginning of each day's outing, the box obviates the need to tie leaders during the fishing day. In the evening after fishing, the box is refilled and made ready for the next day. In effect, the stretcher box acts like a magazine for a rifle, holding the ammunition that might be required.

The box shown on page 116 has been customized by the addition of fly foam in the bottom to hold extra flies and Velcro straps to hold a pipe full of shock tippets.

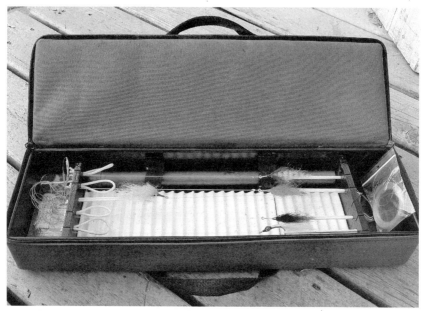

Stretcher box customized with extra fly foam and Velcro straps for shock tippets.

Sunscreen and Sun Gloves

Angling is an outdoor pursuit and exposure to the effects of sun should be taken into account. It is always a good idea to use sunscreen when fishing, but try to avoid getting it on your tackle, particularly your rod grip and fly line. After applying sunscreen, rinse the residue off your palms and fingers.

Holding a fly rod all day, the back of your hands can really take a beating from harmful UV rays. Rowing a boat or raft can do even worse, because the backs of your hands are totally and continuously exposed as you grip the oars. Sun gloves will help. I have used them for years while salt water fishing, but in the last few years I have taken to wearing them for all my fishing to gain some protection for my hands. These gloves block most or all of the UV rays, but are thin enough to avoid becoming an encumbrance while fishing or rowing. You won't even realize you have them on. I keep them in my vest and use them consistently, especially when rowing.

Sunscreen and lip balm will make your day more pleasant.

Sun gloves can save your exposed hands from a beating from harmful UV rays.

Tippet Spool Organizer

Organizing tippet spools can be a challenge. Tippet dispensers of various descriptions are available, but most of them are bulky to carry. For the last few years I have used the Tippet Spool Retainer, a piece of looped elastic material with a clip on one end for attachment to the vest and, at the other end, a removable spring-loaded stopper. To load the device, you take off the stopper, thread various tippet spools onto the elastic and then reinsert the stopper to keep the spools together on the elastic. The tippet spools are handy on the vest so you don't have to fumble in pockets or take a tippet dispenser from a pocket to get at the material needed. The tippet spools stack in order of size, which frees you from having to check the label on each spool. I carry 0X on top, followed by 3X, 4X and 5X, in that order.

Until recent years, most mechanisms for keeping material on tippet spools without unravelling were very poor. Many manufacturers now supply tippet material with small elastic bands that fit around the tippet spool and fill the cavity in the inside diameter of the spool, keeping the material on the spool. The loose end of the material can be trapped in position, available and handy, under the band, elimi-

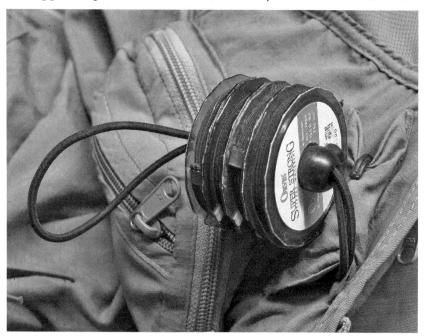

Less bulky than some tippet dispensers, the Tippet Spool Retainer helps you keep tippet spools organized.

nating the need to remove the elastic band. The best of such devices features a small "handle" in the elastic so you can grasp it if you need to remove the band. When the tippet in a spool is depleted, I keep the elastic in case of loss or breakage on another spool.

Binoculars

Small binoculars are handy when fishing. If you think you see rising fish in the distance, the binoculars can help confirm or deny that in short order. If you see an interesting bird or other animal, the binoculars will draw the image closer. If you see birds working an area of the stream, you might even be able to confirm a hatch of insects. I carry a small pair whenever I am fishing and they always prove useful.

Insect Screen

If you have ever attempted to catch a floating insect in your hand, you know how difficult the process can be. When you put your hand into the water, its obstruction of the flow creates a hydraulic cushion just upstream. An insect floating down into that cushion is steered around your hand and pushed further downstream. To overcome this prob-

Small binoculars have many uses when you are astream.

An easily homemade insect screen is useful for catching and examining hatching insects.

lem, I carry a small mesh net in my vest to capture hatching insects and have a good look at them. I made the net by attaching a piece of nylon screening to two chop sticks. By allowing the water to flow on through, the net makes it easy to hold the insect on the screen for examination without the hydraulic cushion effect. Simply immerse the netting downstream from an insect and let the flow trap the insect on the screen, sort of like taking a kick sample (a similar procedure used to collect samples of invertebrate life in streams) in miniature.

Forceps

Of all the tools fly fishers use, probably the most universal is a pair of forceps. These locking pliers are used principally to securely grasp the fly when removing it from the mouth of a fish—or the ear of an angler. Some people use this tool to mash the barbs on hooks, but a small pair of pliers is generally better for that purpose. Mashing barbs

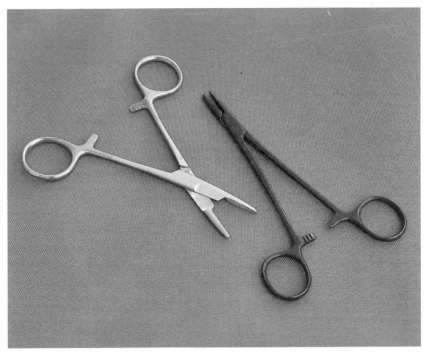

Forceps are the most universal tool of fly fishers, used mainly to securely grasp the fly when removing it from the mouth of a fish— or the ear of an angler.

with forceps, particularly on large hooks, can damage the forceps so they don't close properly. Forceps are also handy for selecting and extracting a particular fly from a fly box. The locking mechanism on forceps allows for wearing them on the front of a vest where they are handy, locked onto the flap of a pocket. Some forceps have flat blades and no cutting surfaces, while others feature serrations on the blades and a cutting surface. I prefer the flat ones, but whichever you choose, a pair of forceps is virtually a required piece of tackle. Some people prefer black forceps, claiming that silver ones set up reflections that could spook fish. That's a nicety that doesn't concern me terribly.

Cradle Net

If you are going to fish for northern pike—particularly big northern pike—one of the best investments you can make is a cradle net. These nets are like mesh eavestrough with handles. When you work the pike near the boat, have your fishing partner slide the cradle net into the water, then you just lead the pike into the cradle. When the fish is

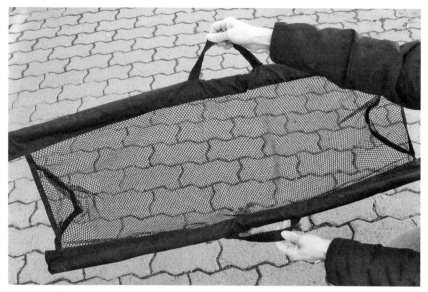

I wouldn't fish for northern pike anymore without a cradle net, which lifts the fish easily out of the water without the thrashing and struggle.

inside, you just lift upwards and the net folds around it. The pike will not struggle and roll in a cradle net as it will in a traditional net. In fact, a pike caught in a traditional boat net is the stuff of nightmares. How do you even begin to get him out? He's thrashing around and eating the net while you only have the tail to grab. With the cradle net, you can quickly remove the hook and slide the cradle net back in the water with one end tilted downward. The pike slides back into the water. I love to fish for pike with flies, but I wouldn't do it anymore without a cradle net.

Line Cleaner

In order to perform properly, fly lines should be cleaned periodically. They do get dirty and if not maintained, they're prone to sinking and sticking in the rod guides when cast. The best line cleaning solution I've ever used is Glide, a product manufactured by the Johnson Wax Company and distributed by Umpqua Feather Merchants (www. umpqua.com). To clean a line, put Glide on the cleaning pads in a line cleaning box, lay the fly line into the groove in the box lid, close

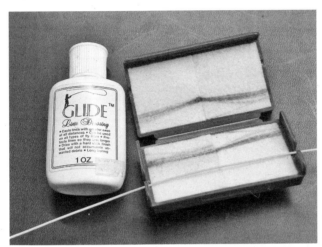

Fly lines should be cleaned periodically or they begin to sink and stick in rod guides when cast.

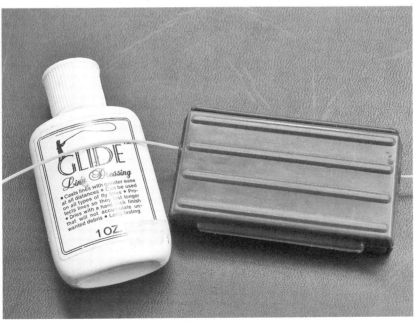

the box then draw the line back and forth through the closed box a few times. When you are finished, buff the line with a soft cloth before spooling it back onto the reel. The line will now be clean and slick and will perform much better for the treatment. For years I understood treating a line with Armor All to be the recommended procedure, and it does make a fly line very slick. However, because Armor All is water soluble, as soon as you put the line on the water the treatment is washed off and rendered ineffective. If you use your lines in salt water, more frequent cleaning is required because salt water imparts a stickiness that causes lines to hesitate in the rod guides.

Reel Lubrication

Over the years I have seen what seem like thousands of fly reels come into the shop for installation of backing or new fly lines. Many of these reels were in deplorable condition, apparently having never enjoyed the benefit of a cleaning. To get the best service and life from a reel, it periodically needs thorough cleaning and lubrication. All you have to do is remove the spool and rinse the frame of the reel in warm water, removing accumulated dirt and debris. Wipe it down with a soft cloth or paper towels and lubricate the spindle with a reel lube, which has less of an affinity for grit and grime than grease. Two other fine products for the purpose are Boeshield T-9, a lubricant developed by the Boeing Company for long term protection of aircraft components, and Barricade, a product by Birchwood Casey intended for lubricating firearms. Both of these products penetrate deeply, displace moisture and dry to a thin, waxy film that protects metal. Any reel worth owing is worth maintaining. If you have a reel that has a cork disc drag, make sure to keep the cork disc lubricated with linseed oil or a similar product to prevent the cork from drying out. If it does, it could crumble, necessitating replacement.

Snips and Zingers

All fly fishers need a snip to cut the tag ends of monofilament that come of tying on a fly or attaching tippet material to a leader. It's very bad practice to use your teeth. The best snips are made of good quality steel, which holds its cutting edge for a long time. The many cheap imitations on the market, made of poor quality metal, do not last long, as they either break apart or become dull. Look for a snip that has a straight cutting edge as opposed to the curved edge you might

Instead of your teeth (very bad practice), you should use a fly fisher's snip to cut tag ends of monofilament. The Zinger retractable pin-on reel keeps a snip handy for when you need it and out of the way when you don't.

see on fingernail clippers. The straight edge lets you know exactly where the cut is made. Most of these snips also have a bodkin in the end opposite the cutter, which is used to clear head cement from the eyes of flies.

Snips are usually attached to some form of retractor, like an Orvis Zinger. The Zinger, which pins on your vest, has a retractable cord that allows you to pull the tool out for use yet will automatically retract to keep the tool out of the way when not needed. These retractable pin-on reels can be used for a variety of tools and the best of them use longer-lived wire cords. "Pigtail retractors," which have a springy, coiled plastic cord, also function well.

Weights

From time to time, fly fishers employ weights to sink flies faster and/ or deeper. Usually these are lead, either tied into the fly or attached to the leader. The most commonly used external weights are either split shot or Twist Ons. Twist Ons are thin strips of lead packaged much like a paper matchbook.

However, as time goes by, the public is voicing concern about the use of lead in fishing, since much of it is lost on snags in the river bottom, causing adverse environmental impact. Some jurisdictions have, in fact, already banned the use of lead in sportsfishing, and it's reasonable to assume more will follow suit in the near future. Whether you share these concerns or not, the salient fact is that lead is on its way out as a mechanism for sinking flies.

Lead-free alternative weights are now available, but most haven't yet earned the approval of the angling community. Tin is one, but will not sink a fly nearly as quickly as lead. Bismuth is another substitute, but is seldom available and expensive compared to lead. So far as I can tell, the best available alternative is tungsten, which is readily available now in the form of beads and cone heads for flies. Tungsten is also quite expensive, but will sink a fly satisfactorily.

I have used tungsten beads for some time in preference to lead. If I am fishing with a streamer or nymph, I will often thread a tungsten bead onto the leader before tying on the fly. When the fly is attached and a cast made, the tungsten bead will slide down the leader to the head of the fly and sink the fly in much the same fashion as a split shot of lead. If the tungsten bead is lost, there's no environmental hazard. When I'm finished fishing with the sunken fly, I remove it and recover the bead from the leader.

Using tungsten beads in this manner is quite within the regulations where lead weights are banned. You should note, however, that some jurisdictions, such as British Columbia, have strict definitions of "fly fishing," and weight of any description added to the leader is prohibited. In that event, tungsten beads can be used in the construction of the fly, but not added to the leader. Check the regulations in force in the area you are going to fish before employing weight in your rigging.

The Tie-Fast Knot Tyer

Nail knots are commonly used for attaching backing to fly line, and for tying leaders or butt extension loops to fly lines. In my opinion, the Tie-Fast Knot Tyer is among the best for tying these knots, which many anglers seem to have particular trouble with. The Tie-Fast tools, which make the nail knot process painless, come in a variety of styles, but they all operate in the same way.

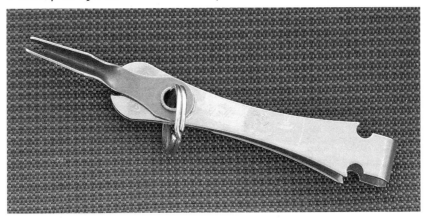

Tie-Fast knot tool

Step 1. Hold the tool in the palm of either hand, with the thumb over the thumb pad on the tool.

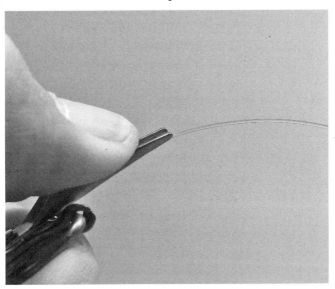

Step 2. Lay the monofilament over the thumb pad and in the channel so that about six inches of monofilament extends past the tip of the tool.

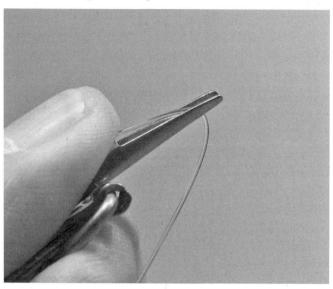

Step 3. Pull down on the monofilament and then wrap the monofilament around the tip of the tool, working back toward the rear of the tool.

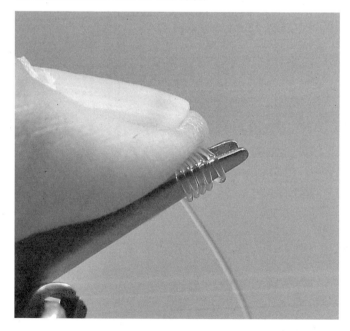

Step 4. After making about five wraps with the monofilament, tuck the tag end of the monofilament through the channel, under the wraps.

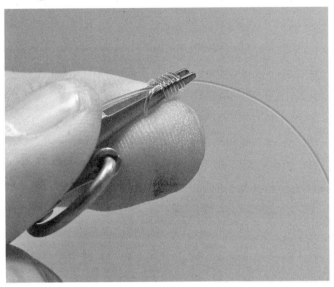

Step 5. Push the end of the fly line into the channel and hold it in position.

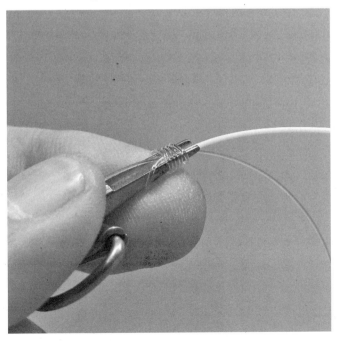

Step 6. Let the wraps slide forward off the tool, trapping the fly line inside the wraps, and tighten the knot by pulling on both ends of the monofilament. When the two ends of the monofilament are tightened, the nail knot is finished. Clip off the tag ends of the line and monofilament closely.

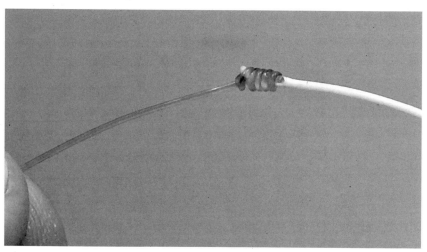

Fly Boxes

All fly fishers use some sort of fly boxes to store and carry flies. Fly boxes are made from various materials, including aluminum, plastic, and foam.

Some of the aluminum fly boxes, such as Wheatleys, are wonderfully well made, but suffer from being heavy and expensive. Most anglers appreciate the workmanship in Wheatley boxes, but they seldom use them in the field.

The most popular fly boxes are plastic, foam or some combination of the two. For floating flies that depend on their hackles for floatation (dry flies), I prefer compartment plastic boxes with some depth, so the hackles do not become crushed or matted. I usually look for boxes with larger rather than smaller compartments; they make it easier to extract flies.

I also like the foam boxes because they are lightweight and virtually indestructible. Their magnetic closures seem perfectly adequate. They also float if dropped in the water. Most foam boxes sport ridges in the foam on at least one side of the box, allowing you to insert a dry fly with its hackles in the "valley" of the ridges so it will not be crushed.

Fly boxes, made of aluminum, plastic and foam, among other materials, are used to store and carry flies. I also find Threader boxes indispensable.

Above: Millstream Box.
Left: Fly Wallet.
Below: C&F Designs Waterproof Box.

Millstream boxes are very popular, with their combination of a rigid plastic frame and foam inserts. They come in a variety of sizes, featuring inserts of both flat and ridged foam. Nymphs and streamers are adequately stored in the flat sides of such boxes, reserving the ridged side for dries.

Some people like fly wallets, usually canvas with a fleece lining. I used to employ such wallets, but eventually set them aside. If they ever get wet, you have to remove all the flies to prevent rusting, and it seems to take forever for the fleece lining to properly dry. Dry flies should not be put into fly wallets.

I also make extensive use of Threader fly boxes (see "How Do I Get A Fly This Small On My Leader?" in previous section). For tying small flies to tippets, the threaders are indispensable. These boxes are also extremely lightweight. C & F Designs Ltd., the company that brought us the threader box, is now making an extensive series of rigid plastic fly boxes that are waterproof, each having a neoprene "O" ring in the frame that seals the box when the clasp is closed. These boxes are beautifully made, though somewhat expensive and a little heavy. Most have "micro slits" in the foam that accept the bend and point of the hook, holding the flies securely in an upright attitude and easing the search for a particular fly. You simply push the bend of the hook into the slit, so the foam is not torn up by the points of hooks. For the discerning angler, I expect these boxes will be popular.

When you are looking at fly boxes, check the hinges on the lid and the closing clasps. Better boxes will have a full wire hinge rather than a two-point plastic one. The closing clasps will be more secure, so if you happen to drop the box, it won't be so prone to bounce open when it hits the ground.

Strike Indicators

In the past twenty years, strike indicators have become standard equipment. These are brightly coloured pieces of various floating materials attached to the leader when fishing with subsurface flies. The idea is to watch the indicator as it floats along the surface of the water and wait for it to do something anomalous in the drift, indicating that the sunken fly has been intercepted by a fish—in short, the fly fisher's answer to bait fishers' bobbers.

Many fly fishers feel offended when strike indicators are called bobbers; but let's be candid, that's what they are. If properly employed, they can be extraordinarily effective. The user must concentrate on what the indicator is doing on the water and be prepared to instantly react when something out of the ordinary occurs. When an angler has difficulty with indicators, it's usually because he or she expects something dramatic. More successful indicator fishers react to subtle variations; they don't wait for a larger event.

Strike indicators come in a large variety of configurations—plastic-covered cork, stick-on foam, pieces of floating yarn and sleeves of plastic fly line that slip over the leader. All are brightly coloured to make them visible on the water.

Of all of the available strike indicators, my preference is for the yarn type. Simple to put on and take off, they're easy to relocate on the leader. They do not interfere with casting and float well, particularly when treated with fly floatant. They alight fairly delicately on

Of all the available strike indicators, my preference is for the yarn type.

the water and are easy to see once there. I don't like cork indicators much because they must be attached to the leader before the fly and can't be removed without cutting off the fly first. They also splash down more heavily and can be a casting nuisance. That is particularly so with some of the larger ones, some the size of cherries, it seems. I don't like the stick-on indicators either, because they are "one-time use only" and then must be discarded. And I don't like the fly line sleeves because they ride very low on the surface film, making them difficult to see.

When you're using very tiny dry flies, it often turns out that the fish has eaten the fly without your knowledge. Strike indicators can help. Tie a small piece of brightly coloured yarn into the leader a couple of feet from the fly; it will be easier to see than the fly. When you see a rise near the indicator, set the hook

A caution: check local regulations before you use strike indicators. Some jurisdictions have prohibited their use. In B.C., for instance, some streams are classified "fly fishing only." On such streams it is illegal to affix anything on the leader between the fly and the fly line.

Gel-spun Backing

Gel-spun backing can very adequately replace braided Dacron backing on your reels. This gel-spun polyethylene material has a significantly smaller diameter than 20# braided Dacron, and that means you can increase your backing capacity on any reel by as much as 60 percent. Even with a smaller diameter, gel-spun backing has almost double the breaking strength of braided Dacron. It's more expensive, but the additional backing capacity it provides has made it immensely popular with salt water anglers. Moreover, it is unaffected by exposure to ultraviolet light, gas, oil or salt. When I first saw the material, I thought the small diameter might lead it to bind into itself on the reel, but that concern proved to be baseless. I've used gel-spun on my salt water reels for several years now. The added capacity is very much worth the difference in price, particularly when using large arbor reels, whose design reduces backing capacity.

And speaking of reel capacity, for some reason (that escapes me) fly line manufacturers generally make their salt water fly lines longer than their freshwater fly lines. In fact, many salt water lines are as much as 15 feet longer. Ponder as I might, I can come up with no cogent reason for this. Even if I concede that average lengths of casts in salt water might be longer than those in freshwater, it still makes no sense. Most people cannot cast the full length of a conventional fly line (90 feet), so to make a fly line longer for salt water use serves no purpose. Most salt water fish run farther and faster than freshwater fish, and generally more backing is required for salt water fishing than for freshwater. In fact, most salt water fish, when hooked, run far enough away to remove the whole of the fly line, whether the line be 90 or 105 feet long, and the backing to line knot is sliding through the guides soon after the salt water fish is hooked. That being the case, I usually cut off the back 15 feet of a salt water fly line and discard it, opting instead for about 30 extra yards of gel-spun backing, which now fits on the reel.

Where Would You Like to Go Today?: Travel Tips for the Peripatetic Angler

Over many years of standing behind the counter in a fly shop, I met literally thousands of anglers who had travelled to the Bow River to fish its fabled waters. I never ceased to be amazed how ill-prepared some were. Most of these fishers did poorly, though they might not have admitted that had anything to do with lack of preparation. And it's not just people coming here that exhibit the phenomenon, it is also our local anglers who travel elsewhere. Here's a typical exchange:

A customer enters the store 30 minutes before closing time and announces he's going to Belize (substitute any destination) to fish for bonefish and tarpon (substitute any target species) and needs some flies, tackle and advice as to how to go about the whole adventure.

"Good for you," says the store clerk, "I think I can help. Have you ever been there before?"

"No," says the customer.

"Have you ever fished in salt water before?"

"No."

"When are you leaving?"

"Tomorrow morning," says the customer. "Can you fix me up?"

Seems preposterous, but this scene, repeated consistently in the shop, is much more common than a customer seeking advice on a trip he's planning six months hence. In fact, so normal has this scenario become that it's almost a surprise when a customer's stated departure time is anything other than "tomorrow morning." I strongly suspect most of these travellers do not have a good experience on their trip.

By not planning ahead to succeed, by default, they plan to fail, and failure becomes a self-fulfilling prophecy. I certainly do not mean to castigate anglers for spontaneity. They'll probably wind up with a less than pleasing result; but that's not my bull getting gored, so, as they say, "Have a nice day!"

The first time I took a fishing trip to a far-flung destination was in 1986, when I joined a group going to Christmas Island in the Central Pacific. As odd as it might sound, one of the things I remember most about that trip was how poorly some people had planned for it. The lesson I learned was that the groundwork you do before a trip will, in large measure, determine its success or failure. Whether you are going fishing in local waters or travelling internationally, pre-trip preparation is the cornerstone on which a memorable adventure is built.

In the years since that first trip to Christmas Island, I have taken dozens of trips to a number of destinations to fish for various species of fish, in both fresh and salt water. Most of the trips have worked out very well, living up to pre-trip expectations. There have been a few busts, but not many. One trip was marred by a guide who, having just been "voted off the island" by his girlfriend, demonstrated less than optimal concentration on the task at hand. A couple of trips have been ruined by poor weather. The worst was getting caught in a hurricane of historic proportions that occurred very late in the normal hurricane season. On the whole, however, I've had marvellous experiences and credit the successes largely to planning.

You certainly can't plan your way around lovelorn guides, but lots of other eventualities, including the weather, can be addressed. I hear you say: "Give me a break. How can you plan around the weather?" Well, for example, avoid the Caribbean junket during hurricane season—June through November. Hurricanes are not a recommended life experience. As of this writing, I've been caught in two. I refuse to be caught in a third, so if you want to go to the Bahamas in August, don't bother calling me.

One of the joys of pre-trip preparation is the anticipation of the journey. Researching the destination, tying the necessary flies, preparing the tackle and planning to succeed have always appealed to me, allowing me to savour the whole experience. Much of what follows is directly related to salt water fishing trips, but the information is transferable to any fishing trip, whether distant or near to home, in fresh or salt water.

Pre-Trip Preparations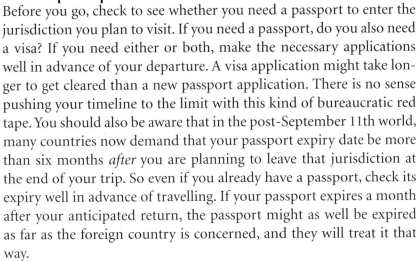

Before you go, check to see whether you need a passport to enter the jurisdiction you plan to visit. If you need a passport, do you also need a visa? If you need either or both, make the necessary applications well in advance of your departure. A visa application might take longer to get cleared than a new passport application. There is no sense pushing your timeline to the limit with this kind of bureaucratic red tape. You should also be aware that in the post-September 11th world, many countries now demand that your passport expiry date be more than six months *after* you are planning to leave that jurisdiction at the end of your trip. So even if you already have a passport, check its expiry well in advance of travelling. If your passport expires a month after your anticipated return, the passport might as well be expired as far as the foreign country is concerned, and they will treat it that way.

After you get the passport, photocopy the pages that show your likeness, the place and date of issue and passport number. This photocopy should be put in a safe place that is not where you store your passport. The photocopy won't take the place of a lost or stolen passport, but will make it easier to get a replacement by giving you all the information you'll be asked for by the replacing authority. Without the photocopy, chances are you won't remember the passport number, place of issue, date of issue and similar details. When my son was travelling in New Zealand, his travelling companion lost his passport and Australian visa. Without a copy of either, it took several extra days of effort before he could continue his travels. Some of that could have been shortened if he'd had the information photocopies would have provided.

Before you go anywhere, gather as much information about your destination as you can. If possible, talk to people who have been there before and get some leads as to what you might legitimately expect. If you are going to a lodge or to fish with a guide, make a list of questions about what to expect when you arrive and ask the questions well ahead of your departure. Don't be bashful about this. After all, you are footing the bills for the trip and deserve to be as well informed as you can before arrival. In truth, the better informed you are, the happier the lodge or guide will be (see insert for questions to ask).

Questions to Ask Lodge Operator or Guide

- What is the typical fishing day?
- Can I drink the water from the tap?
- Will I be wading while fishing or is the fishing done from a boat?
- Is there a telephone/fax number at the destination that I can leave with home in the event of an emergency?
- Is an email facility available at the destination?
- Can my particular dietary requirements be attended to by the lodge?
- Is tipping expected, and, if so, what is the customary amount?
- What weather conditions might reasonably be expected?
- Are there any weight restrictions on baggage or on the number of bags I can bring?
- Are there any medical facilities nearby the destination in the event of sudden emergency or illness?
- Can I be evacuated in the event of sudden emergency or illness?
- Is there electricity at the destination and, if so, is it the same voltage as that at home?
- Are credit cards accepted at the lodge or in nearby towns?
- What is the local currency of exchange and where can you get that currency before arrival?
- What fly patterns are recommended for the area?
- Is the political situation in your destination stable and conducive to visitation without trepidation?
- Will I be met on arrival or will I be expected to get myself to a meeting place after arrival?
- If my airline connections fail, where should I stay overnight if I can't get to the lodge on the appointed day?
- Does my guide speak English?
- How much travel time is involved each day between the lodge and the fishing grounds?
- Can I obtain references for the lodge?

In addition to finding out about the destination, make sure the lodge learns some things about you. If you have any special dietary requirements or allergies to food, medications or insect bites, let the lodge know in advance. Also let the lodge know whom to contact in the event of any emergency that arises during your stay. If you become unconscious for whatever reason, it will be too late to impart such information. Be prepared as well to explain to the lodge operator or guide what you expect from the trip.

Check the timing of your trip. If you want to fish for tarpon and they're not available at the time of year you plan to go, either adjust your planning or adjust your expectations. Be realistic.

On any trip, cost is a factor. Understand that you will pay for what you get, but, more important, you should get what you pay for. If one destination is considerably cheaper than another in the same general locale, you'd best ask why. Consider the following hypothetical case (which, by the way, is a fair representation of a real situation): Destinations A and B are in the same general area, and you'll be fishing for the same number of days for similar target species. Both offer all accommodation, meals and guiding, based on double occupancy in the room and on the boat. Both are adequate accommodation, being clean, well maintained and safe. Destination A charges $2,500 for the junket, Destination B, $3,500. On closer inspection, you discover the following:

Destination A: The guides are relatively inexperienced and do not speak particularly good English. They do not understand fly fishing techniques and cannot cast or instruct casting. They can find the fish for you, but, having done so, their fishing instructions to you are weak or non-existent, owing to a combination of lack of experience and language difficulty. To get to the fishing, you have to first take a car for a 45-minute drive to a marina, then board a boat with the guide for another 45- to 60-minute run to the flats. The trip to and from the flats must be made in the daylight, so the length of the fishing day must be calculated given that constraint. The boats are adequate for travel to the flats, but are not terribly comfortable and are not suitable for poling around the flats when you arrive.

Destination B: The guides are English-speaking and well versed in fly fishing techniques. They can find the fish and walk you through all the steps required to present the fly to the fish. They can explain the nuances of such things as tides, fish behaviour, fishing approaches and tackle rigging. The flats are accessed by stepping out the front door of the lodge or by up to a 45-minute ride in a modern flats skiff rigged for fast, comfortable travel and poling the flats on arrival.

Given these two choices, which is better value? You'll save some money going to Destination A. You will probably have greater success and learn more at Destination B. Is the difference in price worth the difference in the experience? It's your decision, but I know which I would choose.

I'm often asked, "Do I need a guide?" The answer is an unqualified "Yes, you do." If you are fishing in a place unfamiliar to you, to be successful you must spend either time or money. You can spend time learning your way around or you can spend money to have someone show you around. I submit that you're better off spending money on a guide. You can always obtain more money, but no one can give you more time.

Many people are reluctant to pay for a guide, thinking they can do it themselves. Almost without exception, these people are less success-

"He's over there!" Some research about your destination and guides will stand you in good stead.

ful and less satisfied than those who go with a guide. Some refuse to hire a guide for reasons of ego, feeling their skills are good enough to go without. Most are self-deluded. Whatever your skill level, the local knowledge and experience of a competent guide will enhance your fishing experience. I know people who have refused to hire guides (for whatever reasons) and come home declaring a successful trip. I suppose it can happen, but I'm consistently given to wonder how much more satisfying their experience might have been had they hired a guide. I have fished for a long time, I have fished many places for many things, I have reasonably good angling skills—and I always hire guides.

Having hired a guide, listen to what he tells you. This advice might seem self-evident but, believe me, there are people who don't follow it. I have guided quite a few anglers—some competent, some not—who refuse to or seem incapable of following instructions. If you had the good sense to hire a guide, extend your winning streak by listening and doing what he asks.

Do not try to kid anybody about your skills or experience, particularly your guide. If you are a beginner in salt water, that is nothing to be ashamed of. *Everybody* was once a beginner. You are about to embark on a learning curve and life-altering experience. You want your guide to know you're coming to learn. Try to bluff and you'll be discovered the first time you cast a line. If you tell the guide you can cast 90 feet, but deliver only 60, you look like a fool, and the guide will adjust the rest of the script despite what you told him at the outset about your skills.

Be realistic and prepare for the trip as well as you can. If your casting abilities need work, recognize and attend to that before you go. If you cannot double haul, get a lesson and practice well ahead of time so you won't need one on location—an abysmal waste of valuable time, even presuming someone is prepared and competent to teach you. Practice your casting as much as possible in conditions similar to what you might reasonably expect when you arrive. If you are going to salt water, count on it being windy. That being the case, don't relegate your home practice sessions to bluebird days. Learn to deliver the fly on the backcast—invaluable, particularly when you're fishing from a boat.

When you practice casting, keep the number of false casts to a minimum. Any cast can be made with a maximum of two false casts.

For most salt water situations, the time from sighting a fish to the delivery of the fly is about three seconds. After that, the fish will either have moved too far out of range or too close to cast to without being spooked by the fly. Three seconds seems like a short time, but it's sufficient to make a back cast, forward cast, second back cast and delivery. If you insist on making multiple false casts, your target will disappear, and your guide will likely go ballistic.

If there are new knots for you to learn, learn and practice them in advance at home. If you have trouble tying a new knot, get help from a book, another angler or local shop employee.

It is also a good idea to find out as much as you can about your target fish. When I started fishing in salt water, there was virtually no worthwhile resource available. Thankfully, that situation has changed. There is now a wealth of books, videotapes and DVDs on salt water fly fishing. Avail yourself of these as part of your planning.

The internet contains a lot of information about angling destinations. A word of caution, however. Its presence on the internet does not make the information accurate or reliable. Approach it with the same skepticism and common sense you might employ in conversation with a total stranger in a dark bar.

In your planning, be certain to include such things as personal medications. Carry prescription medications in the container(s) that identifies them as such—helpful for customs clearance. Before you travel, tell your physician where you are going. He or she can probably set you up with a small first aid kit/traveller's remedy/preventative kit from office samples. If you are going somewhere really exotic, find out from your doctor or travel advisory authority about any particular innoculations or prophylactic medications. Advanced planning for these is absolutely mandatory; some medications, such as anti-malarial and anti-hepatitis prophylactics, must be taken over a reasonably long span of time preceding your potential exposure to the disease. Regular first-aid items (bandages, etc.) are also handy to have.

Before you go anywhere out of your local jurisdiction, get medical insurance to cover the length of your stay, including in-transit times. The insurance doesn't cost much and will be invaluable if you do become sick or injured. You must obtain insurance before you leave home; you can do this at the same time as you book your flight(s).

I would suggest you also investigate trip cancellation and interruption insurance when you book. Check with your travel agent *before* making any airline reservations or giving a deposit on your trip. It might be that the insurance coverage must be booked prior to giving a deposit on the trip or within a set period of time following the tendering of a deposit, making you ineligible if you delay placing the coverage.

Book your airline reservations early for the best prices and confirmed seating. A travel agent can make the reservations for you and may be aware of seat sales to your advantage. If you have to stay in a hotel en route to your final destination, make the hotel reservations early and get written confirmation numbers at the time of the booking. Keep these numbers handy as you may be called upon to quote them to hotel personnel.

For travel to any destination, your most valuable tool is a comprehensive checklist. If you know anybody who has been where you're going, ask if they have a checklist you can review. If no one you know has been there, prepare a checklist at the outset of your planning. The best checklists result from the following three assumptions: assume the worst eventualities will occur; take anything you think you will need or want with you; and finally, take a spare. Draft your checklist and then set it aside. Revisit it later, and repeatedly, making alterations as they occur to you. Include everything. Rods, reels, lines and flies alone do not a smooth trip make.

Always carry spare eyeglasses and spare polarized sunglasses. If you have only one pair, breakage or loss could seriously jeopardize the trip. I always carry a set of small screwdrivers and spare eyeglasses screws. Losing the temple screw of eyeglasses presents a decided problem. Spare screws can fix that in a hurry. Before you leave on your trip, go to your dispensing optician with your glasses and get the proper sized replacement screws. Most opticians do not charge for this service. Other small tools are handy too, as is a small sewing kit with thread, needle, buttons, safety pins, tweezers and so on.

If you take anything that runs on a battery, such as camera, flashlight or iPod, take spare batteries for each item. If you're really planning ahead, try to select devices on the basis of shared battery type. Then you can interchange batteries in the event of failure. Extra batteries for cameras are a must. Make a practice of reversing one of the batteries in any battery-operated device during travel. Switching the battery poles ensures the device can not accidentally be turned on during the trip, thus draining the batteries.

If you are using a camera on the trip, take more film than you think you might need. If you are shooting digital, take extra memory cards. Extra lenses and a flash can also be useful. I also carry a tripod. A small one is easy to pack and usually sufficient.

Carry a pen. You *will* have to use it during your travels. Wherever you go, somebody will ask you to fill out a form or sign something. Count on it and keep a pen handy. Take small change and small denomination currency with you when you travel. United States currency is generally best. Greenbacks are accepted all over the world. You *will* have to make a phone call or tip somebody. When you do, count on the fact that nobody will have change for a $100 bill—including the magazine or newspaper vendor you pass before boarding the plane. I have been to Belize a number of times. Two Belizean dollars equal one U.S. dollar. If you want to buy a beer and you tender a US $20 bill to the server, you will get your beer and a whole pocketful of Belizean change, which you probably don't really want. You won't receive your change in U.S. currency.

When heading to salt water fishing destinations, carry camera lens cleaning solution. With it you'll be able to properly clean your glasses after they're sprayed with salt water. Simply wiping the glasses off won't do much good; salt water confers a filmy stickiness that requires sterner stuff. Lens cleaning tissues are also a must. The best I have found are pre-moistened with alcohol and packaged in sealed, tear-open pouches. Almost any dispensing optician should have them, and they're inexpensive. Carry a few in your pocket, vest or fanny pack at all times. They're invaluable.

I also carry alcohol swabs wherever I travel. Handy for minor cuts and abrasions, they also work well for cleaning battery connections—a boon when you're in a corrosive, salt water environment. And they're really good for cleaning eyeglass lenses.

Wide cellophane tape or duct tape is invaluable and has a multitude of uses. When packing up at Christmas Island, I discovered a broken zipper on my bag. With the tape I was able to secure it anyway. I have also used tape to lash down stray wires that catch fly line on boat decks. You will find a number of uses for this tape on any trip.

Carry sunscreen and lip balm and use them frequently when exposed to wind and sun. When I am fishing in tropical climates, I usually apply sunscreen first thing in the morning and keep applying it throughout the day. I know of people who have spent most of their salt water trip indoors, painfully recuperating from too much exposure. Never underestimate the power of the tropical sun. Pay particular attention to the earlobes, base of the nose and front of the neck. These susceptible areas can be quite painful when burned.

Carry insect repellent. You might not need it, but if you do, you don't want to be without. If the repellent contains DEET, be careful not to get it on any plastics, particularly fly lines. This stuff can damage a fly line beyond repair in an instant. If the repellent (or any other liquid product you are carrying) comes in a bottle with a flip up lid, fix masking tape to hold the lid closed. I once had sunscreen escape its container en route and the mess in the bag at the destination was unspeakable. You can also place such containers in Zip-loc bags for transit.

Carry a spare. Carry a spare. Carry a spare. Or team up with your travelling companions to ensure they have a spare to lend you when something breaks or gets lost, damaged, stolen, misplaced or dropped in fifty feet of water. Some items to consider:

fly lines (I know of several that have disappeared behind fast moving fish, particularly when the line or backing might run into coral as the fish makes its run);

fly rods (on a trip, rods break for all the same reasons as at home—screen doors, large clumsy feet, overhead ceiling fans and so on); and

rod guides (take both snake and tip guides of various sizes, together with ferrule cement to replace the latter).

For in-transit and after-fishing hours, bring along a book, travel Scrabble or backgammon or some other such diversion. If you are going to a lodge, it's also a nice touch to take small gifts for the staff and guides. A T-shirt or cap decorated with a motif from your home river will be well appreciated by the recipient.

Sample Checklist for Tropical Salt Water Destination

- tarpon rods, 9', #10-12
- bonefish rods, 9', #8-9
- fly reels for tarpon
- fly reels for bonefish
- leader material for tarpon, both class tippets and shock tippets

- leaders for bonefish
- tippet material for bonefish leaders
- tarpon flies
- bonefish flies
- lightweight fanny pack for flats wading
- neoprene wading booties for flats wading
- neoprene cement for repair of wading booties if necessary
- spare backing
- spare fly lines
- reel lubricant
- fly line cleaner and cleaning box
- plastic bags for transporting wet clothing home
- 2 hats with wide brim and neck covering
- safety pins and fly line remnant for securing hat to shirt collar
- knot tools, if necessary
- spare parts for reels, if necessary and available
- rod repair kit with various sized guides, both snake and tip guides
- ferrule cement
- wide cello tape/duct tape
- clippers
- forceps
- hook hone and files
- pliers
- 2 pair polarized sunglasses and sideshields
- eyeglass retainers
- sunscreen, lip balm, sunburn medication
- moisturizer with aloe
- sun gloves
- insect repellent
- toilet kit/personal medication/traveller's preventatives
- soap and shampoo
- flashlight
- first aid kit

- carry bag for fishing gear in boat or on flats
- camera equipment and film
- passport
- notebook or diary
- reading material
- backgammon set/deck of cards/cribbage board/travel Scrabble set
- fly tying kit, if desired
- spare batteries for flashlight and camera
- alcohol swabs
- silica gel packets for camera cases
- waterproof camera case
- US $ in small denominations
- cash or traveller's cheques
- lens cleaning solution and lens tissue
- small tools
- spare screws for sunglasses
- snorkel, mask, fins, if you want to snorkel
- small gifts for guides and lodge staff
- bottle of libation, if desired
- long-sleeved shirts
- long pants
- shorts/swim suit
- T-shirts
- raingear
- socks
- shoes/flip-flops
- emergency water purification tablets

Packing To Go

Luggage

The best luggage to carry is soft-sided, such as duffel bags or the soft-sided variety on wheels. These are easier to pack in small planes, helicopters and boats. While making sure to have everything you may need or want, keep your luggage as light in weight as you can. Remember, at some stage you'll have to carry it. Affix your name and address of destination on the luggage in each direction of travel—one label with the outbound address and one with the return address. That will give the airline a good clue as to your whereabouts when your bag arrives after you do.

Do not use locks on your luggage. Locks need keys, and keys have a maddening habit of getting lost or misplaced. Nowadays, most airline security recommends against locks on luggage, in case your luggage has to be searched. If you want to secure zippers, use plastic cable tie strips, available in any store that deals in electronic gear. These are inexpensive, come in various sizes and can simply be clipped off when you need to open the luggage for inspection or arrive at your destination. The plastic cables won't prevent somebody pilfering from your

A simple cable tie will secure luggage zippers from accidental opening, while allowing airport security access.

bags, but neither will the flimsy locks on luggage if there is a determined thief around. If your cable tie strips are damaged or gone when you next see your bag, you'll know it's been tampered with. In that case, take the luggage to the airline counter, tell them your bag has been opened since check-in and ask them to witness your examining the contents. If the bag has been opened by security personnel, they will often leave a note to that effect inside the bag. If anything is missing, report it to the proper authority before leaving the airport.

Bear in mind that security protocols on aircraft have changed dramatically since the attacks of September 11th. You can no longer carry flies, files, knives, pliers, reels or any sharp object in your carry-on cabin luggage. Carrying rods (even four-piece ones) into the cabin of an aircraft seems to be a thing of the past. If in doubt about any item, put it in your checked luggage to avoid problems. If you arrive at security and they find something objectionable in your carry-on, you'll be forced to forfeit the item or recover your checked luggage to

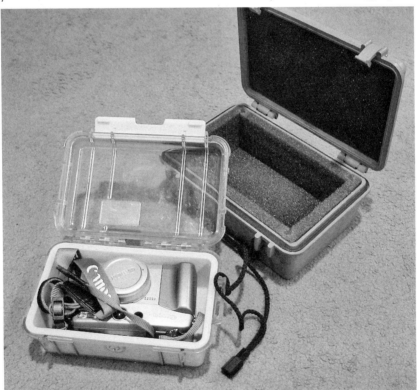

Pelican cases are watertight, dustproof and indestructible—great for cameras and other delicate items.

stow it there. Either way, it's a hassle you don't want. Security protocols are apt to change at any time, so check with the air carrier just before you travel.

If you are carrying cameras or other items that need protection from bumps, jars, rain, sea spray and dust, consider investing in a Pelican protective case. These hard-sided plastic cases, made by Pelican Products, Inc. of Torrance, California are sold in a variety of sizes and colours. They are absolutely watertight, dustproof and indestructible—guaranteed for life against everything except shark attack, bear attack or children under five. Many have a "pick and pluck" foam insert that you can customize to fit any gear you wish to carry. I own several of different sizes and carry them wherever I go. I'm confident my camera will be safe even if the case is dunked in water. I usually leave a small silica gel envelope inside to take care of any moisture that might creep in.

Flashlight

Pelican also makes tremendous flashlights for anglers. They are completely waterproof, have extremely bright xenon bulbs and are, like the cases, guaranteed for life. I know of a particular light, chewed by a Basset hound, that was replaced by the company under the guarantee. I especially like the MityLite, a small flashlight that fits easily into a pocket and is wonderfully bright. Small enough to hold between your teeth when changing flies in low light conditions, it will remain undamaged if dropped, even into water. Some of the latest models feature a clip for attaching the light to the brim of a cap or hat. I carry my flashlight with me after dark in any tropical location. When the sun goes down in the tropics, it really gets dark.

Dry Bags

Another product I always carry is a Seal Line dry bag, made by Cascade Designs of Seattle, Washington (www.seallinegear.com). These bags are made for and used by canoeists and rafters to keep their gear from getting wet. The bags, of pliable plastic construction with a roll-down top and plastic clip closures, are available in a variety of sizes and colours. I use the 20-litre and 30-litre sizes most often. I prefer the see-through bags, which make it easy to locate particular contents without emptying the whole thing. When fishing, I use these as boat bags to carry such items as rain jacket, spare glasses, cameras, film and

See-through dry bags keep contents completely dry while making it easy to locate gear.

spare reels. Even soaked by rain or sea spray, the bags keep everything dry. You can clip the bag's top closure around a seat bracket or upright to keep it from diving overboard.

Clothing and Footwear

Choose clothing depending on where you are going and weather conditions you might reasonably anticipate. Carry good raingear. It will rain, and probably more than you were told to expect. When it rains in the tropics, the ambient temperature is usually pleasant and getting wet is not a problem. However, if you get wet and then travel at high speeds in a boat or truck, you'll chill quickly in the wind created by the moving vehicle.

For the tropics, I suggest you avoid cotton clothing, which get wet and never seem to dry. Clothing made with Supplex nylon is best. It dries quickly when wet and is cooler than cotton on hot days. Long sleeve shirts and long pants give more protection from the sun. You can always roll up the shirt sleeves if you want. The pants I prefer are the "convertible" type, with lower legs that zip off to create shorts. I usually wear a swimsuit or Supplex shorts as underwear. Cotton underwear gets wet and never dries, making for an uncomfortable day.

After a day's fishing, I take that day's clothes into the shower, rinse them out and hang them up. They'll be dry and ready to wear by next morning.

If you are going to be wading when fishing, make sure you have proper wading boots. On salt water flats, the most common footwear is either flats hikers or flat booties. Flats hikers are lace-up boots with hard soles. They're usually tall enough to adequately cover the ankle, and they provide good support when wading. Some flats hikers are sold with a pair of neoprene socks included, but frankly, I find the socks hard to put on and take off. Flats booties are one-piece footwear with a neoprene upper and a sturdy rubber sole. They usually have vertical zipper closures on the sides. Anglers who have tried both tend to prefer the flats hikers because they give better support and protection and last longer in rough conditions, particularly when wading in coral-strewn areas. They are also more expensive. Whichever you use, the boots should close tightly enough at the top to keep sand out, and the hard sole must be sturdy enough to protect the bottom of your feet when wading over sharp, broken coral pieces. When you're in shallow water, footwear with lace closures will work better with some form of gaiter to keep fly line from entangling in the laces.

It goes without saying that your wading boots should fit properly. If you develop blisters from ill-fitting wading boots, your ability to fish will be impaired. On any trip that includes wading, it is of paramount importance to take good care of your feet. Failing to do so can ruin the whole trip. Any blisters, cuts or abrasions on your feet should be attended to immediately. If you get sand or a piece of coral in the boot, stop and remove it before continuing. At some fishing locations you're expected to walk relatively long distances each day, so taking care of your feet is your first priority.

And speaking of wading boots, take special care when storing them overnight. Most tropical venues harbour a myriad of things that wander in the night—crabs, scorpions, centipedes and other such critters—and all of them seem to have a particular predilection for curling up inside wading boots. If you cavalierly discard your wading boots outside the room, you had better be vigilant next morning about checking for trespassers before venturing a toe inside. A land crab in the boot can be a rude surprise, though it won't hurt you badly. A centipede or scorpion, however, is a totally different order of magnitude.

Rod Transport

Some people are paranoid about handing over their rods as checked baggage when they travel, but with today's security concerns, you likely won't have much choice. So get used to it and take some precautions for their safe arrival at the destination. Arguing with airline or security personnel at the airport will not bring about a satisfactory solution to your concerns. I've taken many trips with rods as checked baggage and have had very few problems.

To keep rods safe during travel, make a rod case from 4"-diameter ABS plumbing pipe.

If you are worried about your rods' safety, you might want to consider making a rod case from four-inch diameter ABS plumbing pipe. The pipe is thick-walled, very strong and will protect its contents even should the pipe be subjected to hard use. Cut the pipe to a length to fit the rods, affix a cap with epoxy on one end and fit a screw cap on the other. All the pieces are readily available at your local plumbing store and are not terribly expensive. As a precaution against accidental opening en route, I drive several screws through the wall of the pipe where the lid screws on. One of my cases is covered with a Cordura material and sports a carry handle and "D" rings for the attachment of a carry strap. Eight two-piece fly rods fit inside. I have checked this case on several airlines to several destinations and have had no damage to rods at all.

While You're There

Fishing Set-up and Technique Basics

When you arrive at your destination, the first order of business is to get set up for fishing. Establish a start time with your host or guide. Then ready your tackle for the departure time. Set up your rods, then find a safe place to store them. Many lodges have rod racks handy for this purpose. If the racks are indoors, be careful of the doors when moving the rods in and out of the room. This might seem like nit-picking, but snapping a rod tip in a screen door thousands of miles from the nearest fly shop is more serious than snapping one at home. If there's an overhead ceiling fan in the room, either turn it off or use great caution when moving the rods around. It's easy to ignore or forget a fan, and rod damage can occur in a heartbeat.

When fishing from the deck of a boat, the first item of business is to pull line off the reel and cast to the distance you might have to cast when a fish appears. Now strip the line back, laying it on the deck at your feet. This preliminary is very important because it ensures that the fly line closest to the fly will end up on top of the pile of line on the deck while the line closest to the reel finishes on the bottom. If you merely strip off a lot of line from the reel and pile it on the deck without first casting, the front of the line will be buried under the rearmost portion of the line and your opening cast will probably tangle.

I usually fish from a boat deck in bare feet. If you wear shoes on deck, the line can get wedged under the soles' edges without your knowing—until you try to cast to the target. The wind can push line under your shoes without your even having moved your feet. But, in bare feet, if I'm standing on fly line, I can feel it. Rubber-soled shoes on deck make squeaking noises that are transmitted through the boat's hull to the water, alerting nervous fish to your presence. I have witnessed bonefish bolting like scared coveys of quail from the squeaking on deck. Likewise, be quiet. Do not drop things or scrape them around inside the boat. Those noises are all transmitted.

Directions in a boat are based on the clock. Assume you're at the centre of the clock face. Twelve o'clock is directly in front of the bow of the boat; six o'clock is directly astern. If your guide sees a fish approaching from slightly to the right of the bow, he'll tell you a fish is coming from one o'clock. Similarly, if he sees a fish approaching from slightly to the left of the bow, he'll inform you a fish is coming from eleven o'clock. Point your rod in the direction specified and ask the guide if that is the proper line of approach. The guide will usually let you know how far away the fish is as well.

Before casting, visually locate the target. Salt water flats fish can be difficult to see, but practice helps. After the cast is made, keep the rod low and pointed at the fish. Some guides will even advise the client to put the rod tip into the water to reinforce the low rod attitude. Strip the fly back, making it move away from the fish. Do not stop stripping the fly. If the fly stops, the fish will usually lose interest, ignore the fly and swim away.

When the fish comes in to pick up the fly, strike with the line, not with the rod. Apart from overdoing the false casting, striking with the rod is probably the most common mistake of freshwater anglers who move into salt. The action is inefficient because it does not set the hook well and, more importantly, it removes the fly from the strike zone at the most critical time. Move the rod tip upwards and the fly on the end of the tight line will likewise move up, usually exiting the water and flying into the air as a back cast. Even if the fish were after it, he cannot reach a fly that has been removed. On the other hand, if you strike by pulling on the fly line with the rod tip low, the hook set is more efficient, and, if the fish actually misses, the fly remains there for a second chance. I have seen gamefish miss the fly on first attempt and then securely grab it on the second opportunity. If you attempt to set the hook by raising the rod tip, no second opportunity will arise.

One possible exception is when tarpon attempt to grab a fly and miss it, leaving a large "divot" or "hole" in the water. If you have raised the rod tip and removed the fly from the water, a strike is still possible if you quickly throw the fly back into the hole. When the fly comes back into view immediately, the tarpon will usually grab it, as though it's been looking for the missed fly. Bonefish, however, tend to be spooked by a fly's re-entry and won't usually give you a second chance.

Boat Protocol

When fishing from a boat with a companion, try to establish a protocol around who is going to fish and for how long before surrendering the deck. On a flats boat, only one angler fishes at a time. It's usual for one angler to stay on deck for 20 to 30 minutes or until he has a "shot" (a legitimate opportunity to cast to a fish), whichever comes first. Whether the shot is successful or not, an angler should then remove himself from the deck and let his partner take the casting deck. When not on the casting deck, the other angler helps spot for fish.

When fishing from a boat, the casting angler should be careful not to cast the fly over other boat occupants. For the right-handed angler, the best shot is a fish approaching from the nine, 10 or 11 o'clock positions because it keeps the back cast outboard. If a fish is at 12 o'clock, the right-handed caster can still easily make the shot, mindful that the back cast should be high enough to avoid endangering the guide at the stern. For a fish coming from one, two or three o'clock, the right-handed caster should not make a standard forward cast because that delivery will involve a back cast that whips over the boat and everyone in it. In this situation, the right-handed caster should turn slightly counter-clockwise, make his forward cast high and outside the boat, then deliver the fly to the target on the backhand. The left-handed caster reverses all of the above. So the best shot for a left-handed caster is the fish coming from one, two or three o'clock. And he or she delivers the fly backhand to a fish at nine, 10 or 11 o'clock. Practice this sort of delivery until it becomes second nature. If you are alone in the boat with the guide, make sure the guide knows what you are going to attempt.

Hints for the Wading Angler

When wading to fish, the common practice is to first strip line off the reel, make a cast of the length expected when you encounter a target fish, then strip back all but 20 feet or so of the line. You then recover the fly and hold it in the off-rod hand, leaving some line and the leader out of the rod tip so you're ready to make a cast when a fish is sighted. As you walk in search of a fish, the extra loose line you stripped back will drag in the water and follow you. It's vital to look at the trailing line periodically, making sure it's clear as you move forward. You don't want the trailing line to tangle because, when a target appears, you will need to cast that line quickly and smoothly. It's frustrating when you try a cast only to find the trailing line tangled around your feet, the guide's feet or a coral head behind you. As you move around on the flats, pinch the fly between the thumb and one finger of your off-rod hand at the bend of the hook, with the hook point facing up. When you find your fish, merely release the hook while making a forward roll cast, then move into your backcast and deliver the fly to the target.

Post-Trip Activities

After you return from a trip, make notes about the trip as soon as you are able. Your memory will be freshest at that time and the notes can help immensely in planning your next trip. Haul out your checklist and review it thoroughly. Did you allow for all eventualities? Was there any item or point of planning you missed that would have made the trip smoother? If the checklist is deficient, correct the detail and put it away for consultation before your next trip. Do not defer this chore. Do it while the trip is still uppermost in your mind.

If you have been to a salt water destination, be diligent about cleaning your rods and reels. The salt water environment is corrosive, and you need to do preventative maintenance now, not later. On rods, pay particular attention to reel seats and guides. Wash the rods well to remove any salt residue. I take them into the shower with me and rinse them thoroughly. If the rod has an up-locking reel seat, pay particular attention to the fixed hood on the reel seat. This hood is often hidden under the bottom cork on the rod grip. To remove all the salt, you might have to take an old toothbrush to it. Some people rinse their rods right at the lodge, but in my experience the outside faucets at most salt water destinations spout brackish water. Clean the rods at home where you know the water is fresh.

Check all rods for worn or damaged guides and, where necessary, repair them now. That way, the rods will be ready to use next trip; the maintenance is already done. A friend of mine broke a rod on a trip, failed to repair it on return, forgot about the breakage and then took the broken rod back to the same destination the next year, only to be unpleasantly reminded when he opened the rod tube.

Pay careful attention to your reels as well. Salt water reels are made to be non-corrosive, but they are not bulletproof. They require and deserve maintenance. Almost any salt water species will take you into your backing, which will absorb a certain amount of salt water. When you are done fishing, the water will evaporate, but salt precipitated on the backing could set up corrosion inside the reel. After any salt water trip, I remove the fly line and backing from my reels completely. I store the lines and backing on plastic spools clearly marked as to what line it is and which reel it came from. Next, I disassemble the reels and rinse them thoroughly in fresh water. I dry the parts, lubricate the reels and then reassemble them. I do not reinstall the backing and lines until my next trip. If you ask, your local fly shop might assist you to remove lines and backing. Most have line winding machines that can remove line from the reels. They might also be willing to supply you with spare, unused plastic spools on which to store lines and backing.

Fly lines and flies should also be checked and cleaned after the trip. If you've been fishing near coral, your line's finish may be damaged by coral abrasion and may have to be discarded. Inspect your flies and take precautions to keep them from rusting. If the flies have been immersed in salt water, rinse them well in fresh water and let them dry thoroughly before putting them away. It can be a tedious job, but well worth it if you want to use them on a future trip.

If you've been to a lodge or used a booking agent for the trip, you may receive from them a questionnaire upon your return, soliciting your opinion on ways to improve service. Your input is valuable in helping them make future trips smoother and more enjoyable. I suggest you take the time to complete and return such questionnaires.

Review your photographs and enjoy the afterglow of a successful trip. Planning the next getaway will be easier.

A Final Word

One final thought. If you've never travelled in quest of salt water game-fish before, you are entering a new dimension in angling. In order to be successful, you have to learn some new things, even many new things. That is good. Approach your introduction to salt water as a learning experience and enjoy the ride.

The first time I went salt water fishing I consulted a veteran salt water guide friend. He told me, among other things, that my best trip to the salt would be the third. He explained how the first trip is often filled with mistakes and miscues, occasioned by inexperience and ignorance of the milieu. On first seeing a real, live, six-foot-long tarpon lazily swimming toward your boat, it's easy to turn into 175 pounds of quivering aspic on the deck of a flats skiff. An acute state of excitement and anxiety at the prospect of encountering these legendary animals causes things to go wrong that likely wouldn't were one calmer. You make lots of mistakes, but learn from them. The second trip, my friend continued, builds on things learned in the first trip, and the mood mellows. You are excited, yes, but not to the point of paralysis, and not so much goes wrong. Things start to come together. The third trip, he told me, is the charm. By then, you've acquired a quiet confidence you can function well on command, and your excitement has become more focussed. This time, you get the job done right.

Remember, though, you can't enjoy trip number three until you've accomplished trips one and two!

Do the Right Thing: Fishing Etiquette

The past two decades have seen an explosion of interest in fly fishing and the number of anglers using our streams and lakes. Along with that growth has come, unfortunately, greater potential for conflict among users. All too often we hear stories of ugly incidents and rude behaviour demonstrated by anglers on the stream. As often as not, these conflicts occur as a result of ignorance rather than malicious intent. Like golf, angling boasts a time-honoured tradition with regard to behaviour while astream. Unlike golf, however, no marshals occupy the water courses to remove offenders. Some would say that's a pity. In fact, some would have it that no angling licence should be issued until the candidate passes a test to prove he or she understands the conventions of stream etiquette. Oh that it were so, but it won't happen. Meanwhile, learn and abide by the conventions, and everyone will have a more enjoyable time.

At the very core of angling etiquette is the Golden Rule: "Do unto others only as you would have them do unto you." Were anglers simply to abide by this basic rule, conflicts on the stream would all but disappear. When you encounter other anglers on the stream, consider your actions in advance, with the Golden Rule foremost in mind.

Give other anglers room to fish. You don't like to be crowded when fishing; neither does anyone else. Never enter an occupied pool or run. The first angler there has the right of way, and you should not interrupt. If the place you had wanted to fish is already occupied, either wait until the angler is finished or move along to some other place. If that means you don't get to fish a favourite run on that day astream, it may be too bad for you, but that's the way it is. You would not wish to be imposed upon by a later arrival, so why presume to do the same to someone else?

I was fishing recently with a friend, now in his early 80s, when the subject of fishing etiquette came up. Larry related a story some 70 years old. He and his father were fishing in a pool on a favourite trout stream when a stranger arrived, stepped in the water in front of them, and commenced casting. Larry's father challenged the interloper with a hearty "What the hell do you think you're doing?" The stranger turned and said, somewhat rudely, "What does it look like I'm doing?" Without another word, Larry's father waded over to the stranger and threw a single punch that downed him. After recovering his feet, the stranger departed the scene without uttering a sound, never to be seen again. I guess it's an example of frontier justice that won't be regularly repeated in our more litigious times, but justice it is.

Generally speaking, the angler fishing dry flies is going to start from a downstream position and move upstream. Conversely, the angler fishing streamers is going to start upstream and move down. If you arrive at the stream and see another angler there, watch what he or she is doing and stay out of the way. It's often best to simply move on and leave the run alone. If you don't, you may get your own back from the other guy later in the day.

Never cut off another angler, whether you are wading or in a boat. Never wade in or park a boat in a pool already occupied. The first angler in the pool has the right to the best water first. When approaching the stream, stay away from the vicinity being fished by another angler. You know how angry you'd be if someone blundered into "your" water and spooked the fish you've been trying to catch. Whether an angler is there or not, approach cautiously, because fish often lie near banks and bankside cover.

If you see an angler sitting on the riverbank, assume he's waiting on a rising fish and give him all the room you would were he actually standing in the water. This is particularly true for boaters floating down the river. Give the bank angler lots of room; do not throw a cast in the water while passing. It is really maddening to have a drift boat put down a big fish you've been waiting out.

If you are in command of a drift boat, be observant of bankside and wading anglers. Remember you have the ability to move out and not intrude—be alert and ready to do so. As much as possible, leave the water the wading angler is fishing undisturbed. Pull the boat well away upstream of where the wading angler is fishing and do not cut back in immediately below him. He or she is often stalking a rising fish; don't interrupt the stalk by floating over the fish. Make certain any inexperienced oarsman in your boat understands proper etiquette and abides by the rules. It's no excuse to say your oarsman can not adequately handle the boat. In that case, he or she should not be on the oars in the first place, any more than an untutored driver should be at the wheel of an automobile.

Do not float smaller back channels with the boat. It's not unlikely some wading angler is fishing there. You'll literally have no room to avoid a conflict. Rather, to access a back channel, float to the bottom of the channel, park the boat and walk upstream. Conversely, wading anglers should give boats room to manoeuvre. An angler wading deep and casting into the only channel a boat can navigate gives the drift boat no alternative but to float over the water the wading angler is fishing. When this situation has arisen for me, I've usually said to the wading angler, "I'm sorry to do this to you, but if you gave me any other option, I sure didn't notice it."

I enjoy fishing with friends, but not all anglers want company when fishing. Do not assume anglers want to share their experience, even if you *are* a really good person. A favourite cartoon of mine depicts an angler wearing a large sign on his back that reads: "I am using a size 16 Light Cahill. I am using a 9' 4X leader. I am catching some fish. I abhor conversation when I am fishing." I often recall that cartoon when I'm astream. I'm not against convivial anglers, but recommend you assume the stranger in the stream is less interested in visiting than continuing to fish in relative peace and without interruption.

Speaking of companions, bear in mind the importance of sharing fishing time and water. The best approach when fishing with another is to take turns, particularly if the stream is too small to accommodate two anglers in the same vicinity at once. On such streams, let one angler fish while the other watches, helps to spot fish or offers helpful advice on the best approach. Once the first has had a good shot or hooked a fish, the other gets a turn. As you move up or down the stream, leap frog so that each angler, in turn, gets the first shot at the next unfished pool. An angling companion who continues to outrun you to each new pool, leaving you to fish "used water" all day, may prompt you to look for a new fishing buddy. I certainly would, and, indeed, have done so. If you are unsure about your fellow angler's expectations and method, do not hesitate to discuss them before you get too far along.

Similarly, when fishing from a boat, establish some ground rules at the outset. In a drift boat, the angler in the downstream position usually gets first shot at all the best fish-holding positions. For the angler in the upstream seat, there's a very real element of fishing "used water." Anglers should switch positions regularly. In my boat, we most often fish according to the 20/20 rule. That is, each person is expected to row the boat for 20 minutes or until someone in the boat catches a 20-inch or bigger fish, whichever occurs first. If no 20-inch fish is caught in 20 minutes, everyone in the boat changes position. The oarsman moves forward to become the downstream angler, the person in the front of the boat moves to the back and the angler in the back becomes the oarsman for the next 20 minutes or until a 20-inch fish is caught. When a large fish is caught, whoever caught the fish takes over the oars. The person in the back moves to the downstream seat and the oarsman becomes the fisher in the rear. Though this might sound somewhat complicated, long experience has persuaded me it's the best way to share the fishing time. Another wrinkle in the scheme sees us play "three strikes and you're out," on top of the basic 20/20 rule. That is, if you have three encounters with fish during any 20-minute period (e.g. strikes that are missed or fish that throw the hook), you take over the oars as though the time had expired or you'd caught a large fish. Another twist: the oarsman always has first shot at any rising fish encountered on the drift. The boat is stopped to allow for wading and fishing to the rising fish, and the oarsman gets first try.

Set your own rules, but I would suggest you establish them and make sure they're understood in advance. If all agree on the procedure at the outset, there should be no hard feelings later over unequal fishing time. In the final analysis, all of these suggestions really just come back to the Golden Rule. If somebody is discourteous to you on the stream, do not reciprocate. That takes you to the lowest common denominator and everyone's enjoyment is ruined. You might politely point out a breach of etiquette to an offender, but an argument can really ruin a good day astream, and if you're dealing with a complete yahoo, an argument is what's coming. Over the years I've had a number of distasteful encounters on the stream. The rudeness coefficient, it seems, is always high and the shine invariably taken off the day. I've decided the best course is usually to just walk away. There is other water to fish.

Now, about the term "Frenchman's Creek." Frenchman's Creek is a conception of the late, great angling author Robert Traver, a.k.a. John D. Voelker. He called every stream he fished Frenchman's Creek to camouflage the real name and thus conceal the location of his actual fishing venues. Lots of anglers have their own Frenchman's Creeks—spots, incidentally, they might have spent considerable time and effort to find— and are prepared to jealously guard these locations to prevent them being overrun by hordes of anglers. If someone, including a professional guide, takes you to his or her Frenchman's Creek, you've been entrusted with a confidence you should respect. Please, do not reveal the location to anyone. And don't go back without the permission or in the company of your original "host." Your companion revealed the secret presumably because he or she thought you'd enjoy the place. The *quid pro quo* is that you keep your mouth shut about it. Return there without the person or permission and you breach that confidence. And if you take someone else with you, so much the worse. Before you know it, that person will, in turn, do his buddy a favour and so on, until one day you arrive to find the stream crowded with strangers. When that happens, you too may become a little more secretive about your favourite fishing spots, but it will be too late for that particular Frenchman's Creek. While it is true trout streams need friends to maintain and protect them, "kiss and tell" anglers are not generally the most desirable kind.

GLOSSARY

Angler – a fisherman. The term arose from the practice of bending a needle to an angle and using the resulting tool to impale fish.

Anodized – in reference to a fly reel, a protective layer or coating applied to the reel by electrolysis, which protects the reel from corrosive elements in salt water.

Anti-reverse reel – a reel with a built-in clutch mechanism that allows the spool of the reel to release line while the handle of the reel remains stationary.

Aquatic insect – an insect that spends all or part of its life in water. Mayflies, caddis flies, stoneflies, dobsonflies, dragonflies and damselflies are examples.

Arbor – the centre post on a fly reel spool that rotates around the reel spindle. Fly line is recovered by wrapping it around the arbor of the reel.

Attractor – a type of artificial fly that is usually bright in colour and/or flashy and is not representative of anything particular in nature. Fish are thought to grab attractors as a result of curiosity, aggression or territoriality. The Royal Coachman pattern is considered typical of attractor patterns.

Backing – reserve line that is wound onto a fly reel before attaching a fly line. The backing lengthens the available line, so an angler can stay attached to a large and/or strong fish that runs further from the angler than the fly line is long. Backing is usually made from braided Dacron or gel-spun material.

Blood knot – a knot often employed to attach tippet to a leader.

Class tippet – an intermediate section in a big game leader which lies between the shock tippet and the butt section of the leader. The class tippet has the lowest breaking strength in the leader.

Clinch knot – a knot commonly employed to attach an artificial fly to tippet.

Dampen – the action of a fly rod when it returns to a straight condition after being flexed. A properly designed fly rod will do so quickly without vibration. Rods that don't dampen quickly are difficult or impossible to cast properly.

Desiccant – a substance, usually made with a silica gel base, which dries out or removes moisture from a sodden fly. Silica gel is hydrated silica in granule form.

Direct drive reel – a reel whose handle is attached directly to the reel spool so that one revolution of the handle causes the reel spool to make one revolution. Also known as single action fly reel.

Double taper – a fly line made to be finer at the ends and thicker in the middle, or belly. A double taper is the same taper and diameter moving from the mid-point of the line to either end of the line. This style of taper is quite old, conceived when fly lines were constructed of silk. Silk lines would not float unless treated with a silicone-based paste. Since the line tapered equally from either end to the middle, the angler could tie either end to the backing and attach a leader to the opposite end. During the course of the fishing day, the waterproof paste would wash off the portion of the silk line being used. When the tip began to sink, the angler could remove the entire line from the reel, retie the now wet tip to the backing, attach the leader to the still dry opposite end and fish with a freshly greased line for the rest of the day. When manufacturers began making lines of plastic, the double taper should have disappeared into history, but did not because some consumers still demanded this taper for their fly lines, reasoning that, with a double taper, they had two lines in one. Damage one end or wear it out and one could simply swap the line end for end. While this sounds good in theory, I do not know very many anglers who actually do this in practice. Their fat belly causes double taper lines to take up much more space on a reel spool, thereby limiting backing capacity. Unless you increase the size of the reel to accommodate the double taper line, the end nearest the reel arbor is wrapped into a very small diameter. Left there for an extended period (which most usually happens), it might never straighten when you do attempt to turn it around. Some people argue that a double taper line lands on the water more delicately than a weight forward taper line of the same weight, an argument, in my estimation, that is completely specious. The taper charts from line manufacturers show that the front 35 feet of a weight forward line has exactly the same taper as the front (or rear) 35 feet of a double taper line. They differ only past that point. With the same taper through the portion of line most often cast, how could one present with more delicacy than the other? Apart from Spey lines, a form of double taper line, double taper lines are an historical anomaly. A double taper line may facilitate longer roll casts and, when the belly of the double taper is on the water, may load the rod more efficiently than a weight forward line of equivalent length.

Drag – as pertains to fly reels, an adjustable mechanism built into the reel that introduces friction (tension) and allows fly line to slip from the spool smoothly and evenly while preventing the reel spool from over-running; or as pertains to artificial flies, when the artificial fly travels through or over the water at a speed faster than the current. This acceleration occurs when the fly line is stretched over water moving at a different speed than that where the fly is resting. Some portion of the fly line may be pushed downstream faster, forming a "belly" in the line that skids the fly through or across the water.

Dry fly – a fly that floats; a floating fly that imitates a variety of adult insects, both aquatic and terrestrial.

Dun – a sexually immature adult mayfly, also known as a subimago.

Emergence – departure from the water of aquatic insects that have reached maturity. Having developed wings, they fly away from the water for a period of time before mating and ovipositing. Also known as a "hatch."

Ferrule – the joint that attaches one section of a fly rod to another.

Floatant – a hydrophobic substance, usually of silicone base, applied to floating flies to waterproof them so they will float higher and longer.

Floating Line - a fly line made to float through its entire length when placed on the water. Floating lines are designated F.

Flag – in reference to rod manufacture, a long, wedge-shaped piece of graphite cloth wrapped around a mandrel in the construction of a rod blank.

Graphite – a generic term for a type of man-made carbon fibre used in the construction of fly rods.

Guide – a spiral or circular wire attached to a fly rod, through which the fly line passes and is funneled up the rod. The guide might be a stripping guide, the large guide closest to the handle; a snake guide, a spiral-shaped wire guide found along the rod blank; or a tip guide, cemented at the tip end of the rod blank; or a person who holds himself out as knowledgeable about fishing in a particular area and offers to share that knowledge with an angler for a monetary or other consideration.

Hackle – feathers used in tying artificial flies.

Hatch – see Emergence.

Hook keeper – a small bent wire or circular ring found immediately in front of the rod handle intended to hold the fly in place when the rod is being moved from one location to another.

Hook size – the size of a hook according to the Redditch Scale. During the early 1700s Redditch, a city in Worcestershire, England, was the needle-making capital of the world. Similarity of manufacture quickly led to Redditch becoming also the fish hook manufacturing capital of the world. Hook-makers standardized hook sizes, based on the "gap" or distance between the point and shank of the hook—the latter being the long aspect of the hook extending from its eye to the start of the bend. A size 1 hook (#1) had a designated gap, a #2 had a slightly smaller gap, a #3 had a slightly smaller gap than a #2 and so forth. The higher the number, the smaller the gap. Over time, usage eliminated all sizes designated by odd numbers other than #1, and today hook sizes smaller than #1 are designated #2, #4, #6, #8 and so on down to #32, a hook so small it has no eye. Therefore, in hooks *smaller* than a #1, as the number of the hook increases, the size of the gap (and the diameter of the wire the hook is made from) decreases. A #14 hook is smaller in gap than a #12, but larger than a #16. Hooks *larger* than #1 are designated by an "aught" and a slash. A hook slightly larger in gap than a #1 is #1/0. Hooks then proceed upwards in size by designations of #2/0, #3/0, #4/0 and so on up to #8/0 or even larger. There is a relationship between the size of the hook employed and tippet size. (See Leaders in "What You Need: Basic Tackle.")

Larva - a sub-adult stage of development in the life cycle of an insect between the egg and the pupal stage.

Leader – a tapered length of clear material (monofilament or fluoro-carbon) that is used to separate the fly from the fly line in order to conceal the line from the fish. The thick end of the taper (the butt) is attached to the end of the fly line, and the thin end of the taper (the tippet) is attached to the fly. Leaders are tapered by extruding the material through a die or by knotting together decreasing diameters of material. Such knotted leaders are known as compound leaders.

Line weight – a system of demarcation for fly lines constituted by the American Fishing Tackle Manufacturers Association in 1961. The system, which establishes a standard for the casting weight built into the front 30 feet of fly lines, assigns a number between 1 and 12 to the line. The lower the number, the lighter the line. Line weight is measured in grains.

Lining a fish – casting a fly line or leader close enough to a fish's location that the fish is frightened by it.

Loop – in reference to casting, the loop is the large, horizontal "J" shape made by the line in the air during casting. Loops are said to be "wide" or "open" when there's a large distance between the loop's top and bottom and "tight" when a small distance. A tailing loop occurs when the top of the loop falls beneath its bottom and in the process ties knots in tippets, leaders and even fly lines. Tailing loops are the result of poor casting technique.

Mandrel – a cylindrical, tapered steel rod employed in the manufacture of hollow, tubular fly rod blanks.

Matrix – as pertains to rod blank manufacture, a system of resins that holds graphite cloth together.

Multiplier reel – a fly reel that contains a mechanical component(s) that causes the reel spool to turn at a higher revolution rate than the handle to which the spool is attached.

Nail knot – a knot commonly used for attaching backing, leader material or butt extensions to fly line.

Nymph – a sub-adult stage of development in the life cycle of an insect (in some insects referred to as a larva); or an artificial fly designed to imitate same.

Ovipositing – an egg-laying flight by aquatic insects.

Presentation – the delivery of an artificial fly on or into the water.

Pupa – the stage in the life cycle of an insect between the larva and the adult. In this stage the insect does not usually move or feed, but it undergoes significant changes on its way to becoming an adult. An example of a pupa is the chrysalis, or cocoon, stage wherein a caterpillar transforms into a butterfly.

Putting a fish down – frightening a fish by some kind of inept approach, like clumsy wading, falling in, casting a shadow over the fish or poor casting. Once a fish is put down, it will not feed for some time because safety always trumps feeding. A fish that is frightened cannot be caught by any legal angling means.

Reel seat – the component of a fly rod that allows for the attachment of the fly reel.

Rod blank – the hollow, tapered shaft which constitutes the basic form of the fly rod, to which is added guides, handle and reel seat.

Rod butt – the bottom end or section of a fly rod, where the grip and reel seat are attached.

Rod tip – the thin end or top section of a fly rod.

Shock tippet – a wire or heavy monofilament section attached to the front of a leader used to prevent fish with sharp teeth or abrasive mouths from abrading or biting the fly off the tippet.

Shooting line – in reference to casting, the act of releasing fly line on the forward casting stroke, allowing the line to lengthen or extend to a target.

Single action reel – see Direct Drive Reel.

Sink tip line – a fly line manufactured to sink in its forward end, while the balance of the line floats on the surface of the water. Sink tip lines are designated F/S.

Sinking line – a fly line manufactured to sink through its entire length when placed on the water. Sinking lines are designated S.

Spare spool – an interchangeable component of a fly reel that holds the fly line and backing, and which is inserted into the frame of the reel.

Spinner – a sexually mature mayfly adult, also known as an imago.

Streamer – a group of artificial flies that are meant to imitate minnows, fry, leeches and other organisms that live in water and swim as a means of locomotion. Such flies are often called "bucktails" when tied with hairs rather than feathers.

Stripping guide – the large rod guide nearest the handle of the rod on the blank.

Stripping line – the act of retrieving fly line by drawing, pulling or jerking the line back toward the angler.

Surgeon's knot – a knot commonly used to attach a tippet to a leader.

Taper – in reference to fly lines, the shape of the line, the shape and diameter of the line; in reference to a fly rod, the diameter of the rod blank.

Terrestrial – an insect that spends all of its nymphal and adult life on land; or a fly that imitates such an insect. Grasshoppers, ants, butterflies, wasps and bees are examples of terrestrials.

Tip Guide – the wire loop at the tip of the rod through which the fly line passes.

Tippet – the thin, terminal end of a leader to which a fly is attached; or a piece of level diameter monofilament or fluorocarbon material attached to the end of a tapered leader to extend its length.

Weight forward – a fly line conformation in which the line tapers in its front 30 to 35 feet, but beyond remains a consistent thin diameter to the end of its running line. The running line must be attached to the backing on the reel and the leader must be attached to the front of the weight forward line. Weight forward lines are designated WF.

Wind knot – a small overhand knot in a tippet, leader or line, normally caused by improper casting.

Window – a term used to describe the area through which a fish can see objects above both up to and through the surface of the water.

ACKNOWLEDGEMENTS

I wish to thank my *companeros* Dennis Hall, Mike Gifford, Homer Spencer and Russ Webb for their encouragement and advice in the preparation of this book. And special thanks go to my friends Bob Knight, Jennifer Buck and Jeff Petersen, whose enthusiasm through this process was always uplifting. All of them were imposed upon, sometimes mightily, to read all or portions of the manuscript in its various iterations. For their efforts I am most appreciative. I also want to thank my wife, Linda, for her patience in allowing me the time and space to finish this.

NEIL L. JENNINGS is an avid outdoorsman who spends a great deal of his time hiking around in the backcountry with a fly rod, a camera and a tripod, recording the beauty of the landscape in southern Alberta and British Columbia. For much of his adult life he was a fly fishing retailer in Calgary, Alberta, Canada. He fishes extensively, in both fresh and salt water, and has taught fly fishing related courses for over 20 years. Neil is the author of four previous books, *Trout Flies of Alberta and Southeastern British Columbia; Uncommon Beauty: Wildflowers and Flowering Shrubs of Southern Alberta and SoutheasternBritish Columbia; Prairie Beauty: Wildflowers of the Canadian Prairies and Alpine Beauty: Alpine and Subalpine Wildflowers of the Canadian Rockies and the Columbia Mountains.* He and his wife, Linda, live in Calgary, where they have resided for over 30 years. They spend a lot of time outdoors together, chasing fish, flowers and, as often as possible, grandchildren.

Alpine Beauty

*Alpine and Subalpine Wildflowers of the
Canadian Rockies and the Columbia Mountains*

by Neil L. Jennings

Alpine Beauty explores the wildflowers and flowering shrubs
commonly found in the subalpine and alpine environments in
the Rocky Mountains of western Canada. Due to harsh weather
conditions, the plants that exist at higher elevations are generally
different than those at lower elevations. In this environment,
low shrub and herb communities become the rule.

ISBN: 978-1-894765-83-1
Price: $22.95
Pages: 212 pages. 5" x 8". Paperback
Illustrations: colour photos throughout

Wildflowers of the Canadian Prairies

Neil L. Jennings

Prairie Beauty

Wildflowers of the Canadian Prairies

by Neil L. Jennings

Prairie Beauty explores the wildflowers and flowering shrubs commonly found in the prairie environment of western Canada. Written for the enjoyment of all who venture outside and wish to identify the wild flowering plants they encounter, the book is directed at readers with little or no background in things botanical.

ISBN: 978-1-894765-84-8
Price: $24.95
Pages: 236 pages. 5" x 8". Paperback
Illustrations: colour photos throughout

Uncommon Beauty

Wildflowers and Flowering Shrubs of Southern Alberta and Southeastern British Columbia

by Neil L. Jennings

Uncommon Beauty explores the wildflowers and flowering shrubs of a large area from Jasper down to Creston, over to Glacier National Park in Montana, and up through Lethbridge and Edmonton. Extensively researched by author and outdoors enthusiast Neil L. Jennings, this guide will inform and intrigue the reader, while also assisting with plant recognition and identification.

Exceptional photographs of over 200 species of flowering plants, plus information about each plant, make Uncommon Beauty the ideal field guide for hikers (and amblers) of all skill levels. For ease of reference, the book is arranged by flower colour and by plant family. A complete index is included, using common and scientific names for all plants.

ISBN: 978-1-894765-75-6
Price: $22.95
Pages: 256 pages. 5" x 8". Paperback
Illustrations: colour photos throughout

NOTES